I'VE BEEN AROUND

By the same author

Maiden Voyage

I'VE BEEN AROUND

TANIA AEBI

Foreword by
Bernadette Bernon

SHERIDAN HOUSE

For Nicholas and Sam, my family, my friends,
and sailors everywhere.

Published 2005 by
Sheridan House Inc.
145 Palisade Street
Dobbs Ferry, NY 10522
www.sheridanhouse.com

This book is based on articles previously published in
Latitudes and Attitudes magazine and *SailNet*.

Library of Congress Cataloging-in-Publication Data
Aebi, Tania
  I've been around / by Tania Aebi.
     p. cm.
   ISBN 1-57409-213-8 (alk. paper)
    1. Aebi, Tania—Travel—Anecdotes. 2. Sailing—
Anecdotes. 3. Sailing—Philosophy. I. Title.

GV810.92.A43A3 2005
797.124'092—dc22   2005018500

Edited by Janine Simon
Designed by Keata Brewer

ISBN 1-57409-213-8

Printed in the United States of America

Contents

Foreword vii
Introduction xiii

PART 1. Is There a Difference?

Guys 3 ⌒ Seriously Sirius 7 ⌒ Small Difference 11
Strength 14 ⌒ Close Call 17 ⌒ Pirates 21

PART 2. On Board

Barefoot 29 ⌒ Swimming 33 ⌒ Overboard 37
Kitchens 41 ⌒ Christmas 44 ⌒ Overkill 48
Simplicity 52 ⌒ Superstition 57 ⌒ Water 60
Trash 64 ⌒ Relief 68 ⌒ Goodbyes 72

PART 3. Contretemps

Lessons 77 ⌒ Precision 81
Fouled Prop 85 ⌒ Pride 88 ⌒ Squalls 92
Life Rafts 96 ⌒ Perfect Storm 100

PART 4. On Location

Volcano 107 ⌒ Lake Champlain 111
Withdrawal 114 ⌒ Procrastination 118 ⌒ Greece 122
Antigua 126 ⌒ Shipping Ashore 130

PART 5. Words

Bugs 137 ⟶ Jackspeak 141 ⟶ Bowline 145
Nomenclature 148 ⟶ Catalog This 152

PART 6. Characters, Kids and Cat

VARUNA and Tim 157 ⟶ VARUNA and Nicholas 161
Michel 165 ⟶ Effort 168
Brian and Betty 171 ⟶ Tarzoon 175

PART 7. Bearings

Intuition 181 ⟶ Cashola 185
Provisioning 189 ⟶ Tides 193

PART 8. Home Is the Sailor

Photo Ops 199 ⟶ Homecoming 203
Picture This 206 ⟶ Fantasea 210

Foreword

Twenty-one years ago, at the Annapolis Boat Show in Maryland, a curly-haired girl named Tania Aebi noticed my *Cruising World* name tag—at the time, I was the magazine's managing editor—and shyly said hello. Her father stood nearby urging her on like a mad conductor, while, with some hesitation, she told me she was going to sail around the world. Alone. It was that last word that riveted my attention. She looked no more than 12! She was 17, she said. I asked her if she had a boat. She did, she said, a Contessa 26 that she and the mad conductor were fitting out here at the show. "I want to be a writer," she told me. "Writers need something to write about, right?"

"Well, there's a lot more to writing than just having something to write about," I said. "Bluewater solo sailing is dangerous. Have you ever sailed anywhere by yourself?"

"No," she said sheepishly. "I only just learned how. But Daddy says a lot of ninnies have sailed around the world, so he thinks I'll be able to do it." I looked over at Ernst, a wild-haired guy who was nodding and grinning. I remember thinking, what kind of family is this?

Tania wrote a story for me about sailing with her dad, an eccentric Swiss artist, across the Atlantic on a boat he'd bought on a whim, after reading about sailing in a magazine while sitting on the toilet in a friend's bathroom. On that hair-raising voyage to New York, he and his three kids learned about sailing together, the hard way, and he and Tania talked about her future. She was adamant about not wanting to go to college—she hated school at the time—and wanted to travel. Ernst was equally adamant. He wanted her to get serious about something after high school, and wouldn't foot the bill for her to lark around the world aimlessly. But he would be willing to spend her college money on a sailboat, if—and this was a big if—she would use it to do a significant voyage, alone, and write about it. "Why not?" she said.

Indeed. In my job, I'd heard lots of loony ideas from all kinds of well-meaning people. Normally, these ideas never got off the ground. But this felt different somehow. This kid was going to try it, and her father was egging her on. A few months later, I went to New York to be there for one of her shakedown sails, and to take photos. What I saw was a frightening display of confusion and sailing inexperience that kick-started all my maternal instincts. I ramped up my worries about her safety, and told Tania time and again that she didn't have to go. She could bag the whole crazy idea. Nope, she said, she was in too deep, and was pressing onward. The photos of Tania casting off from New York show a withdrawn girl in tears. The next stop was Bermuda.

I jumped on a plane a few days later, to meet her in Bermuda at the end of her first passage, which should have been a five-day voyage, six at the most. Day after day, I waited in St. George, biting my nails. She didn't show. Other boats that had departed the East Coast days after VARUNA were coming into the harbor, reporting clear weather and speedy passages. Tania was nowhere to be seen.

Finally, after almost two weeks at sea, VARUNA arrived with a thinner Tania, an exuberant Tania, a Tania bubbling over about the passage, and about how she'd been lost out there, and most likely sailing toward Canada, until she'd taught herself celestial navigation underway, and got back on track. The rest is sailing history, the epic story of the youngest woman to sail around the world alone, chronicled in the most popular series of articles *Cruising World* ever published, and in the best-selling book she wrote, *Maiden Voyage*, which I had the privilege to co-author with her. Behind the scenes of that larger-than-life adventure was another tale, the private story of Tania's apprenticeship as a writer, and the growth of our friendship.

When Tania first started writing her series of features for *Cruising World*, they seemed to me far more formal than she herself sounded. They lacked the terrific humor, self-deprecation, and disclosure that, in person, were some of the most charming aspects of her personality. Over a short time, together, we soon developed a way to pull those aspects out of her, and integrate them into her articles. In addition to writing each article for *Cruising World*, she'd write long letters to me—a girlfriend—with all the funny observations, and casualness, and gossip, and honest disclosure of her fears and feelings. With her permission, I'd take these "letters" and her articles, and marry them all together. The result was all Tania, and magic—the pure innocent voice of a girl becoming a woman, experiencing life and love from the deck of a sailboat.

During Tania's two-and-a-half-year voyage aboard VARUNA, we always stayed in close touch through letters and phone calls—indeed, everyone at *Cruising World* knew that if Tania called collect, they should accept the call and find me, no matter where I was or what I was doing. Then we'd talk for ages about the things girls talk about, and then I'd ask her questions about different aspects of the story she'd just sent in, and we'd talk through and enhance different sections. We both loved the process. When she came home to be with her mother in New York, who was dying of cancer, I went to New York to be with her. My own mother had died young in the same way, and we had that tragedy in common.

When Tania sailed to Gibraltar, her last landfall before sailing trans-Atlantic and home, I flew there too, to help her however I could, to ready her for the gigantic media blitz awaiting her arrival in the States, and to put a satellite transmitter aboard VARUNA so we'd know where she was in the ocean. She ended up tending to me as much as I to her, as it turned out, after I was robbed of all my money, passport, and luggage in Spain. One month later, by the time VARUNA and an exhausted Tania sailed into New York Harbor to the cheers of thousands of people lining the docks to greet her, *Cruising World* was receiving up to 300 calls a day from worried readers frantically trying to find out if Tania was home yet, and safe.

In the year that followed, Tania moved to Newport, Rhode Island, where I was living, and we began working on the book about her voyage. She and Olivier rented the basement apartment of my dad's house, where they got married, and I was Tania's maid of honor. When I wasn't working at *Cruising World* during the day, Tania and I were together late into almost every night, hammering away on the Macintosh computer that we'd bought together, talking and writing, making tea, talking, telling family stories, writing, making notes, talking, making changes, writing, singing songs, and always talking. Together we knit the story, committed to the idea that this should be more than a sailing tale, more than the recounting of an adventure—that it should be a real story about a life.

At the onset of the book project, I was the driver, pushing for a certain structure for the chapters, pushing for disclosure of so many of the personal things that I knew had happened, pushing for unfolding the story in as intimate a way as possible. We would talk through a chapter, then while I was at work during the day Tania would write essays on different subjects that would be contained in that chapter—for instance, what a night out in Greenwich Village was like as a punk rocker, or how the worst hour of a certain storm felt, or what life with her mother was like. Then I'd come over in the evening and weave parts of the essays together, write the bridges between them, and then she'd edit the chapter to make it sound true. It was an overly laborious process at times, and intense, but it achieved our goal of creating a book that was all Tania. By the time we finished the project, our roles had slowly reversed. It was Tania who was driving, Tania who was writing. She'd found her footing, her voice, and her confidence. The book was hers.

We were delighted when *Maiden Voyage* did so well in hardcover, over the moon when it made the *London Times* Best Seller List, newly excited every time it was translated into another language and published in yet another country, thrilled when it was named as a Best Book For Young Adults by the American Library Association. Through the years since then, our lives have evolved and criss-crossed. Tania moved to Vermont, had two sons, built a house, and life, and—stop the presses—went to college and graduate school after all. I went on to became *Cruising World*'s Editorial Director for 10 years, married a psychoanalyst with wanderlust named Douglas, and embarked on our own sailing adventure, an exploration of the coast of Central America aboard our boat, ITHAKA.

Unlike Tania's VARUNA, my ITHAKA is fitted out with most of the modern conveniences of navigation. These days, whenever I check our electronic charts, or download weather data through the single-sideband radio, or check the radar for shipping in the middle of a black and squally night, I sometimes stop and think of Tania sailing across the same oceans as I am now, in her little cockleshell of a boat, with only a sextant to guide her, and a cat named Tarzoon for company. When I imagine that, I'm more awed than ever about what she accomplished at such a tender age.

When I think of Tania now, however, I rarely think of her as one of the icons of sailing lore, even though she most certainly is that. I think of her first and foremost as one of my dearest friends, a friend who always inspires me. She helped me make my own writing better, less flowery, more spare, clear, and honest, and for that I'll always be grateful. She demonstrated by her actions that there's almost nothing we can't do in life, once we set our minds to the task. She showed me that there may be great risk in going it alone, but that to spend time with yourself is a critical ingredient in the process of self-awareness, taking you to places you never dreamed possible, and in the end making you appreciate what it is that you want to come home to. Oh, and one more thing. She was absolutely right those many years ago. If you want to be a writer, then push out beyond the life you know, read voraciously, try things that are beyond your experience, see the world, then find the home and loved ones where you belong, so you can write about all you've seen, and all you've learned along the way.

Bernadette Bernon
June 2005
Isla Tupsuit Dumat
San Blas Islands
Panama

Introduction

It was one of those perfect October weekends on the western shore of the Chesapeake, the fair weather a gift to sailor and non-sailor alike. At the 1997 Annapolis Boat Show, a fresh breeze blew the smells of salt, pitch, and pilings around vendors, booths, and spars, whipping up a symphony of clanging halyards to the accompaniment of squawking seagulls cavorting overhead. A radiantly blue sky surrounded a sun casting its autumn glow over shiny hulls and tents, glinting off buffed stainless steel railings, bronze portholes, and twinkling wavelets in the harbor.

Crowds were streaming past the entrance gates, swarming on the docks with their sun visors and sunglasses, shopping bags, laughter, and snippets of nautical jargon: RPM, range, draft, beam, spinnaker, sheet, fid, and baggywrinkle. The ambiance smelled and sounded authentic and boaty, nothing like the artificial, fluorescent-lighted, climate-controlled, fiberglass and carpet fiber itchiness of other boat shows held in indoor convention centers. Annapolis was the only boat show that didn't give me a rash.

The boat I was on flew a large banner advertising the new enterprise I was launching with my friend Jill, a venture that was reintroducing me to the sea in a whole new way, a business way. Boat shows were necessary for drumming up interest, so for four days, Jill and I handed out flyers, took down names for the mailing list, and promised adventure and everlasting memories to anyone who joined one of the ten-day sailing vacations we had lined up for France, Greece, and Thailand.

Meanwhile, down the dock on a floating, astro-turfed platform, another fledgling business, a new magazine for sailors called *Latitudes and Attitudes,* was marketing itself. On day two, during a lull in the action, Jill grabbed me, saying, "I've got someone you have to meet."

She led me to the magazine's current headquarters where Bob Bitchin, the all-in-one editor, founder, and publisher, and his wife, Jody, were busily taking down information from a line of new subscribers. Jill and I stood there and watched, waiting for a good moment to cut in and introduce ourselves, using the time to size up sizable Bob.

He was like nobody I had ever seen working a boat show, where clean cut khakis, deck shoes, polo shirts, and baseball caps are *de rigueur,* a uniform that helps salespeople not sell boats to one another. Well over six feet tall, Bob's unruly hair curled around a jovial, bearded face atop a massive body. And, I mean massive. Everything about Bob was big. He had big hands, big feet, big ears, big jewelry. He was one big canvas.

His fingers were encrusted with golden rings and every exposed bit of flesh was covered with tattoos, spreading northward from ankles and wrists to thighs and upper arms, where the multi-cultural artwork disappeared under clothing. Even on this crisp autumn day, Bob was wearing nothing but shorts, his trademark Hawaiian shirt, and Teva sandals. In time, I came to realize this was the only outfit he ever wore, even when sailing the freezing waters around the Greek Islands and New Zealand. While everyone else was bundled up and shivering in foul-weather gear, sweaters, and hats, Bob was comfortable in his shorts, shirts, and skin.

His energy generated enough heat to always keep him warm, the energy that had led him from a previous life as a Hell's Angel and publisher of biker magazines, to one of the cruiser, with his own boat and a new rag for other cruisers. Beside him, it was easy to see that Jody was also filled with the boundless energy that enabled her to keep up with him, though she was more seasonably dressed in trousers and a *Latitudes and Attitudes* sweatshirt proclaiming their credo: *The only difference between an ordeal and an adventure is attitude.* At first glance, Jody appeared diminutive, but only because I was seeing her in comparison with Bob. Actually, she was about the same size and weight as I, which could be called average. Together, they made quite the driven team destined to bring *Latitudes and Attitudes* soaring right smack into the middle of the sailing market.

Ever the more outgoing one—in our business relationship, Jill was marketing, I was reservations—when finally, there was a break in the action, Jill walked up to Bob and made the introductions.

"Hey, I read your book," Bob said to me. "Loved it. How about if you write an article for us, something that might help your business?"

"Sure," I answered, immediately liking them, their look, and rallied to their attitude. Squelching self-doubt-fueled reservations, I said. "I'll give it a shot."

Soon after I returned to my home in the Vermont hills, and Bob and Jody reboarded their boat doubling as home and office in a Los Angeles marina, I fired one off, the first one. I wrote about the road I had been traveling since completing my solo-circumnavigation and writing the book about it, the journey that had eventually led me to the boat show. The article was published in the eighth issue of the bi-monthly magazine and then, my phone rang.

"Hey," Bob asked. "How about if you do a column for the magazine? We'll call it *There Is a Difference*. It can be about cruising from the female point of view."

"Sure," I replied, again. "I'll give it a shot."

As the magazine mushroomed in size and readership, because Bob and Jody are amazing businesspeople with a vision, I gave it one shot after another. My business failed because I didn't have a business-like bone in my body and too many reservations, while my sailing career went through several transformations, but I kept writing for them. Casual and friendly in its approach to the sailing world, the magazine's tone provided me with a place to explore my own reflections on what I already knew and continued to learn about the mariner's way of life, and how to share it all with others. Bob gave me total freedom to take my essays in any direction I wanted, allowing me to discover I had a thing or two to say, not just about sailing, but about the world in which I am raising my two children.

I kept up with Bob's deadlines, even as *Latitudes and Attitudes* went monthly, and for a couple of years, I also helped run their Share the Sail cruising vacations, which were based on the same model as the trips I had given up managing on my own. Months passed and one day, six years had gone by and I pulled the pile of past issues down from the shelf above my computer to go over the subjects I had already covered to avoid repeating myself. To my surprise, I saw a considerable collection of essays had grown out of the first article.

"Hey," I thought. "Instead of letting all these words languish in past issues, how about if I gather them together and turn them into a collection?"

So, I gave it a shot and came up with the following, unreserved selection. I hope they are as much fun to read as they sometimes were to write.

I'VE BEEN AROUND

PART 1

Is There a Difference?

Guys

⁓

I had to travel over seven thousand miles to get a story about a guy with an attitude that fitted the title of my column: There is a Difference. I didn't know the guy's name, but, for the sake of this piece, and because he was French, I called him Guy. Guy and I crossed hairy eyeballs at a bareboat charter base on the French Polynesian island of Raiatea after a trip during which we sailed to Taha'a, Huahine, Bora Bora, and back.

Flitting among these landfalls in paradise for ten days, I spent many idle moments visualizing the dock at home base and the moorings in front of it, walking myself through the mechanics of backing in and tying up. On our last day, I briefed everyone on my boat about the upcoming procedure, assigned duties, and got all the lines and fenders ready in advance of the big moment. As we approached the base, a Tahitian fellow came out to meet us, tied his dinghy alongside, jumped aboard and proceeded to fuss with everything, which was what he got paid to do. Since, until his arrival, the boat had been my contractual responsibility, I helped him, even though he didn't talk much and seemed intent on doing everything himself. When I asked if I could dock, he hesitated, then let me. I did it perfectly, swinging the stern around until it was lined up with the other boats before backing in. That was when I saw the reason for his hesitation.

Standing on the next boat over was the irritated-looking

Guy, some sort of authority figure flanked by several nervous Tahitians watching this chick try to do what they normally did. As soon as we were within jumping range, they were all over the boat, grabbing the wheel, the lines, and control. My job done, I stepped aside and let the four of them finish. They tied bow, stern, and spring lines as if they were racing a clock and bracing the presidential yacht for a hurricane. Then came Guy's wing-dinger: "See," he said in French to the poor kid who had come out to help us, "that is feminine pride," sneering, as if my wanting to dock the boat were a bad thing.

Au contraire, mon frère; Guy's own pride couldn't allow for a French-speaking American, and I happen to be one. But, unfortunately, I am incapable of thinking up perfectly biting, split-second retorts, in any language. The French even have a word for this: *l'esprit de l'escalier,* staircase wit, something you only think of on the way out. "Hey, I understood every word you said," was as snappy as I could get on the spot.

Mildly flustered, he returned with vague comments about insurance, responsibility, and what a pickle I would have been in if the docking had gone awry, totally missing the point that as far as dockings went, mine was pretty good. For the next couple of hours, we glared at each other while the group disembarked, and we waited for inventory and equipment check-out to be completed before our rides to the airport arrived. That was all the time I needed to formulate the perfect answer, but only in my head. Feminine pride, my foot, I wanted to say to Guy, and never did. What the heck is that anyway? Could it be something that would actually give me enough nerve to argue with a control freak outside the safety of my imagination?

My kind of pride gets a boat back to the charter base clean and in as good of a working condition as when it left, and it feels hurt by undeserved criticism. Yes, I am proud of my docking ability, and what's more, it's fun. In Raiatea, bringing the boat in to the dock had much less to do with gender than with simply wanting to end a great trip by nailing a final stern-to docking, a nautical icing on the cake. I'm sure even Guy feels the same pride about docking well, because many sailors do. But, for him, I was also the American female, a sub-species, which probably drove him to pick the raspberries off my cake.

Even though I love doing it now, docking wasn't always my favorite thing. The idea of nearing a dock with an unwieldy sailboat terrified me for many years because of inexperience and audiences like Guy. Harbors and marinas attract onlookers, and docking typically guarantees a place in the headlight, which is never a good place to practice anything tricky. I refined the art of dodging the worry associated with pivoting, approaching, backing in, and pulling away from docks in front of the inevitable other Guys. I got really good at anchoring and dinghying long distances, and once safely tied up to shore, I hated to leave. I managed to get pretty far in the world of sailing without ever really understanding the complexities of propeller, rudder, and directional relationships, which became a major thorn in my side. This was no way to live on a boat, no secret to bear alone, but it seemed easier than taking the initiative necessary to fix the problem.

I squeaked by during the years when I was only responsible for me and my own. Everything changed when I began leading charters, where docking ashore must happen whenever possible. My first trip was with a group in Corsica and Sardinia and I can't forget the embarrassing spectacle I choreographed in different harbors with the stern swinging wildly, Guys hollering, and other boats warping us in with bow and stern lines. On my second trip, which was in Greece, I had a major breakthrough on the largest boat (47 feet) I had ever captained and with six passengers who were expecting to learn from me.

Island hopping in Greece meant that every morning we left a dock and every evening we approached a new one, where there is only one way to dock: stern-to the quay. The anchor gets dropped and the chain gets eased out while the boat backs into a spot in a very straight line so as to not run over any other anchor chains. Anchoring and docking all at once! It seemed impossible, and my first attempt inspired a sympathetic local captain to give me some instruction.

The lesson in broken English I got from this Greek Anti-Guy who slid matchboxes, lighters and cigarette packs around on a taverna tabletop to illustrate what had to happen was all I needed. With a cigarette hanging from his lips, he explained right- and left-turning propeller effects, thrust, the coordination that must happen between the anchorperson and the helmperson, and backing and filling. I finally got it during that trip, and learned how to execute the granddaddy of maneuvers under power, the Mediterranean mooring. Propellers, tillers and docks never intimidated me again, and this meant a lot for my self-confidence and pride.

Calling it *feminine* pride doesn't make any sense to me when we're only talking about a good or a bad docking. I'm sorry I didn't set Guy straight. But a girl can only hope that someday, somebody will let Guy know that yes, there is a difference, and it has much less to do with Venus and Mars than it has to do with attitude.

Seriously Sirius

Living in a house on the northern fringes of hilly New England, I am completely boatless. I don't even own a canoe, which would be nice on all the rivers and lakes we have around here. The only real significant sailing I do these days happens on charter boats, and at the end of the ten-day trips, I hand over the keys, a list of problems the temporary boats may have had, and get on the airplane that brings me back to these hills. Home again, I may be without a boat, but the parallel floating universe out there, and the people who live in it, often feed some memory that bugs me until either it gets sorted out, forgotten, or written about.

Recently, the three boats in the group I was sailing with pulled in behind a perfect little sandy islet at the entrance to a large bay for an overnight. It was our last anchorage on this particular Caribbean charter and it was beautiful; the sun was setting in an orange sky behind a group of small rocky islands to our west and gray smoke drifted limply across the calm water from the mainland, bringing evening smells of roasting food. One of our boats had already anchored in the midst of a cluster of other boats and wanting to be close, we dropped our anchor off their bow and reversed. The holding was poor and we dragged for a while before hooking. With my head down in the anchor well, I coaxed out a bunch of reluctant chain before looking up to see if we were too close to a nearby cruising boat. Oh, no. There it was, a peculiar vessel that had distinguished itself by boxing in the entire cockpit with a plastic and fabric structure, and it was about fifteen feet away. We had to move.

Our boat was equipped with the most cantankerous windlass and filthiest chain and I was loath to pick up and re-anchor right away without being positively sure the current arrangement wouldn't do. So, I hesitated for a moment and stood on the foredeck, arms akimbo to keep hands dripping with gunk away from body, waiting to see if by some chance the boat would swing and settle into a better position. It didn't look good, and as the engine rumbled in neutral, I scanned the anchorage for a better spot. I was just thinking we could try again on the other side of our friends' boat when a head, followed by the upper half of a browned male figure, leaned out from a crack in the plastic and fabric contraption next door.

"You're not serious, are you?" he said.

"Excuse me?" I answered. What was he talking about?

He reworded the query which seemed so stupid I thought I'd heard wrong. "You're not staying there, are you?"

Oh, man! Was this commentary from the peanut gallery the price for a moment's hesitation? It was already a pain to have to anchor again, and the last thing I needed to hear was this guy's thinly veiled criticism. Maybe he was just playing around. Still on good behavior, I explained, "We were just trying to get close to our friends."

"Oh, that's nice," he said, sarcastic and humorless.

"No," I sputtered, completely taken aback, "What's nice is to be nice."

So there! It is so frustrating when the perfect comeback doesn't occur when it would be most effective. Annoyed by this fellow and angry at my sluggish wit, I turned to the disgusting anchor chain and started hauling. As it came up, link by filthy, splattering link, I fumed. What an unfriendly schmuck! The engine was running, I was standing over the windlass, all was calm, and there was nothing anyone on our deck had been doing to give anyone else the impression we were satisfied with our anchoring. All we had been guilty of was a hesitation born of reluctance to do an unpleasant job on a beautiful early evening, and this guy felt he needed to do some chiding. Out of the corner of my eye, I saw him smugly retreat back under the cover of his cockpit as the anchor came up and we motored around to the other side of our friends, hooking on the first try, and swinging free without any more fuss.

Later, I realized what had happened. With his comments, the man was placing us in the pecking order where charterers come beneath cruisers. All he had seen was a charter boat full of ignoramuses who needed some rebuke from a more seasoned and knowledgeable cruiser. Ha! How well I know the impulse. I, too, once looked upon charterers condescendingly, back in the days when I was young enough to think being a cruiser could make me superior. I can remember regarding fleets of Beneteau-type sloops as lightweight carriers for a world of part-time, uncommitted bareboat sailors who will never know what it's like to call a real boat home, the work of it day in and day out, in season and out of season.

Cruising boats and charter boats share the same waters in many charter-friendly parts of the world, but there the similarities end. Cruising boats are floating, self-contained homes that tell their own stories. Paint jobs, deck equipment, names, nationalities, and flags tell so much about the dreams, miles laid under the keel, experience, and the commitment that comes with the lifestyle. Even the goofiest cruising boat reveals a story textured richer and deeper than what any charter boat can ever aspire to.

Meanwhile, charter boats are self-contained hotel rooms that give nothing away beyond what lies on the surface, simply because nothing is there that isn't on a whole fleet of other identical boats. There are very few clues to guess at the stories that exist within, and the outward appearance of any charter boat can never do more than hint at the level of experience and capability aboard. Charter boats are like books with no covers.

Who knows what had brought my anchoring critic to take our coverless book at face value and assume we couldn't anchor because we were a charter boat? Maybe he had just had an unfortunate encounter with a more cloddish group. Maybe he was gun shy and figured he needed to put us in our place before something bad happened. Maybe he hadn't learned about the dangers of making assumptions based on very little information.

Maybe then I could have quipped my way out of the dreaded pigeonhole, putting him back in his place by reinterpreting his initial question. I could have understood what he asked as: "You're not Sirius, are you?"

Then, I could have answered, "No. Actually, I'm Polaris, the center of your universe."

How would that have been for placement in any pecking order? Now, maybe instead of wasting time thinking up the perfect retort, I could be gazing at my hills, still boatless, assuming he got it.

Small Difference

What's good for the goose is good for the gander. Or is it? Let's start with the bane of my own existence, one whose annoying potential is magnified ten fold in the self-contained environment of a boat. In one word, it is: hair.

Hair on the head, hair on the legs, hair anywhere, as long as it grows, refuses to be ignored. As far as the hair we don't want to lose goes, it needs to be maintained and cared for to avoid turning into a haystack of bleached out and broken split ends. This becomes a tall order when shampooing is accomplished with salt water, or the day after a freshwater shower has been relished, the do gets subjected to thirty knots of wind and flying salt spray. It takes a small arsenal of conditioners and careful maintenance to keep hair looking good at any length other than a buzz cut. And that's just head hair, and men everywhere could peevishly say they need to pay attention to their own as well. But, how often do you hear a guy bemoaning his split ends?

Okay, fine. Let's assume men do care a little for head hair. Leg and underarm hair also need to be addressed, too, however, especially for those of us with hirsute genes. Unless he is a diehard bodybuilder or an avid cyclist, a man doesn't need to consider hair removal below the neckline. He can get away with a beard on his face, and even come off looking salty. But, woe is the girl with hairy legs and a smidgen of vanity. I speak from experience on this battlefield. It is no small matter.

While we have an impressive array of hair removal techniques at our disposal in this country, it gets reduced to some pretty basic stuff "out there." And, since most cruising tends to be done in the tropics where bare legs are exposed rather permanently during waking hours, this becomes an everyday issue, unless you prefer long skirts and pants to shorts. Also, maybe it's just me, but I find it very uncomfortable to go swimming directly after a shave, and when this becomes a daily chore, then swimming is never fun, which isn't such a good thing if you live aboard. It's sort of like being a woodworker allergic to all tropical wood.

This hair problem was brought to a head for me many years ago in Polynesia. There, not only were many of the women ravishing, but they were completely hairless, except for where it counted—above the hairline, which made me feel even more self-conscious about the plight of my legs. For two years up until that particular landfall, I had been trying the *au naturel* look, long and flowing, like a song from the *Hair* soundtrack, with some bleaching help. But, have you ever seen roots on leg hair? I have. It's not pretty, and because of the smooth-skinned Polynesians, I started shaving again. Quickly, the novelty of svelte, flawlessly tanned legs was replaced by the ordeal of two stinging shaves a day in port, with a bucket on deck, keeping a baby step ahead of the prolific growth. Only on passages can you let things go.

When a friend on another boat recommended waxing, the disposable strips she gave me to try ended up not being as easy to replace as canned corned beef and tarps on most of the planet in the eighties. If I waited for the hair to grow long enough, duct tape worked passably well. One French girl told me she used melted sugar, but she had about twenty hairs on her legs. A woman on a boat just has to figure out what works best for her.

Here's another point to consider: where there is hair, you will find hairballs and dust bunnies. While dust bunnies in a house can be whimsical rascals floating into discrete corners and under furniture, in the damper sea environment, they just stick their gross little selves anywhere they please, usually on something white—white cockpit soles, up against white coamings, or in the corners of white countertops. And, never, ever do they miss the head, the four-star venue for any self-respecting hairball.

Now, I know both men and women have hair. Men are just as apt to have luscious ponytails, and their body hair can be significantly more impressive in quantity than on females, but this leads to another difference: who cares more where the hair goes once it parts company with the host body? There may be a few guys out there who do scoop out the shower drain, who do brush their hair overboard, and who aren't able to pass by an errant wad without picking it up, but for the most part, I'd venture to say this is a rare breed. If you find him, imitate him, swell the ranks. The ones I've known prefer to fix a clogged bilge pump rather than monitor and maintain the disposal of lost hair.

It's all about losing hair, intentionally or not. If we're looking for differences between the sexes, the hair conundrum is the most obvious to me. As for finding other differences, give me more time to think about it when I'm not managing hair.

Strength

The subject of strength often comes up in panel discussions and conversations about boats and a woman's place aboard. This preoccupation with what the absence or presence of strength means usually leads to lengthy debates full of doubts and questions that often have little to do with reality. Apparently, many women don't feel confident about their own physical prowess, hence their usefulness or ability as crew is limited. Why does this perceived requirement for Herculean force grab so much of the attention? Curiosity, resourcefulness, and determination are the real issues here and a dearth of these is what will make or break any cruising dream for a man or woman, not strength.

Lack of strength never led to disaster on any of the boats I've sailed, from two-and-a-half years sailing alone aboard a 26-footer to numerous charters on boats ranging from 38 to 60 feet. I am not Charles Atlas, by any means, yet any situation that could have been handled better in hindsight has always been due to lack of knowledge, fatigue, or cocksureness. The American poet James Russell Lowell wrote, "In the scale of the destinies, brawn will never weigh as much as the brain." Walk up and down the docks of any marina. What you will see clambering about on the decks is not a line up of future Olympians, but a ragtag selection of every body type, age, and gender.

Far more important than being well-stacked, and what most

happy and confident sailors have in common, male or female, is some basic knowledge about sailing in general. Nobody needs to be an aeronautical engineer, master navigator, skilled mechanic, or neurosurgeon before stepping foot on a boat. However, familiarity with basic plotting, sail handling, motors, and safety definitely comes in handy.

Recently, I read a book by a woman who bumped into a hurricane during a delivery with her boyfriend. In the middle of the Pacific, they rolled 360 degrees, the boyfriend went overboard, and she was knocked out for more than a day while the furious tempest subsided. She came to, alone, dismasted and over a thousand miles away from any land. She jury-rigged a mini-mast and foresail and plotted a correct course for Hawaii. And, judging from the pictures and her own descriptions of herself, she was no amazon. Just a regular woman caught up in a very irregular situation with some preparation. Her survival was solely due to prior curiosity about how things other than the stove worked, and learning celestial navigation.

Some of us learn well from books, applying what we read to reality. Others need to go out and create messes and generate their own theories. For every person who fastidiously reads the manuals before tackling a project, there is another who flings the manual aside and barrels right in. Either way, no matter how we go about it, we are never poorer for the experiences that teach us how to write our own manuals.

Also, modern age has been accompanied by all sorts of inventions, some great, some not so great. Among the useful are roller-bearing winches, windlasses, and the old reliable block and tackle. Strength rarely takes precedence over wit and learning how to use and maintain these simple mechanical advantages on a reasonably sized boat.

This shouldn't be breaking news to anyone with some common sense, and a common sense approach as routine practice in sailing will always outweigh the benefits of hefty biceps. Cruising as a lifestyle is a choice, and to make it work, so is the acquisition of knowledge and a persistent inquisitiveness. Therein lays the potential for real strength.

Hercules or not, the playing field has never been so balanced for men and women. Laurence J. Peter, the author of the "Peter Principle," said, "Most hierarchies were established by men who now monopolize the upper levels, thus depriving women of their rightful share of opportunities to achieve incompetence." It isn't strength, but knowledge that will breed confidence and ultimately the ability to relax and enjoy cruising for what it is—a pretty good thing that is possible for anyone with a bit of determination to learn.

Close Call

Totally becalmed after thirty days at sea, I was ready to do anything to get to land. About fifteen miles off Sri Lanka in the Indian Ocean, the wind died completely during the night. Morning found me bobbing there in middle of the shipping lane, nervously watching big hulks zoom past while glimpses of distant mountains shimmered in the heat of the rising sun. This passage had taken far too long, family back home would be worried until I called, and I wanted nothing more than a decent meal, a cold drink, and some people around me. When my ears picked up the sound of a small engine, I eagerly scanned the glassy water for its source.

A fishing boat materialized in the hovering haze and took shape as a brightly colored local vessel with curlicue Singhalese writing on the prow. I waved at the two men aboard, clad only in some tatty fabric wrapped around their waists, and they smiled, slowed down, and drew up alongside. One of them held onto VARUNA's railing, keeping an arm's length between the two hulls rocking in the oily swell. They spoke no English, I spoke no Singhalese, but with sign language I managed to make them understand a tow toward land and out of the shipping lane would be very much appreciated. Soon enough, my boat was tied behind theirs, and one of the fishermen had invited himself into my cockpit. He sat there and stared boldly at this young girl alone on a sailboat who had appeared from a distant land across the sea. As grateful as I was for the tow, I also began to feel a little uneasy.

Here were two guys with a few nets, hooks, fishing line, an old boat, and some scraps of fabric for clothes. Here was one girl with a nice fiberglass sailboat, and all kinds of clothes, books, electronics, and food. Even though, by American standards, I was under-equipped, next to these two guys, I could have been piloting the GOLDEN VANITY. Comparing our two rigs would be like comparing apples and Buicks.

Fourteen years ago, Sri Lanka belonged to a part of the world where people scrambled to be the first to greet sailors coming ashore with their bags of garbage. Scraps of paper, bits of plastic, string, jars, and cans—you name it—became in a very poor country a bounty of items to recycle into many other uses. For a nanosecond, I thought my boat without me aboard might recycle much better than any bag of trash, and what could stop this from happening? Having been incommunicado for the past thirty days, there wasn't a single person other than these two guys who knew exactly where I was. There was nothing to stop less-than-honest fishermen from succumbing to temptation at the cost of one girl's existence.

I've only played out this alarming scenario in hindsight, for it had nothing to do with what I really felt on that day. Sitting in the cockpit with a staring stranger and his colleague guiding us, I was barely conscious of the vague worry; it was overshadowed by a joyful giddiness that became more pronounced with every mile made good toward land. Instead of discomfort, I felt immensely grateful to these guys who were going out of their way to help. I plied them with gifts. I dug out T-shirts, fabric, old magazines, some money, and a bottle of rum I was never going to drink. I even gave them my address. I remember a lot of smiling, sign language, and mutual staring, until suddenly, still miles away from the harbor, they let me go and puttered off to their homeport up the coast. Still becalmed, I was sad to see the first live humans I had talked with in over a month leave, and disappointed because they hadn't towed me in any closer.

Then and there, preoccupied with the challenge of catching every land breeze to get into Galle by nightfall, I had no idea that, in future years, I would describe this encounter as a "close call." Since I'd been a female on a small boat, sailing alone across oceans to many different countries, I was later often asked if I was ever scared for my life because of other people. For lack of anything more sensational, the hours spent with the Singhalese fishermen became the story to tell of how I may have come close to something bad once, but didn't. I suffered at the hands of adverse weather conditions and the nature of boating in general, I'd reply, but, in the two and a half years I spent on that trip, and in my subsequent travels, both alone and with groups, I had nothing worse to offer. Even in Sri Lanka, the worst only happened in my imagination, I'd say, and this is so because we live on a planet where good people outnumber bad.

In a way, cruisers must be more open to cultivating this faith in human nature, and this was what allowed me to regard the fishermen's presence as assistance rather than danger. As I once did, cruisers are still arriving in harbors everywhere on their boats, often with all their worldly possessions contained within one hull. Over and over again, they are being absorbed and welcomed by people of entirely different cultures, socio-economic backgrounds, religions, and ways of life. Even though sometimes it seems as if the bad, or the potential for bad, gets more of the attention, it hasn't really kept the number of boats out there from growing. Ever since Slocum wrote about his adventures, others have been following in his wake, cruising the oceans, and collecting the colorful memories of relationships and interactions ashore that will follow them through life.

Then one year ago, and thirteen years after the day I was becalmed off the Sri Lankan coast, I got a letter from one of the fishermen. He still couldn't speak or write English, but he had made the effort and paid the price for a letter writer to make

contact with me. He had found my address, he said, and remembering the day and wonder he felt at finding me on the
ocean inspired him to find out how I was doing now. Did I have
a husband and children? Was I happy and healthy? He sent news
about his boat, his friend, his own family, and said he was looking forward to hearing back.

I was simultaneously thrilled, ashamed, and thankful. It was
thrilling to hear the song my memory sings of Sri Lanka was
also being sung by the memory a Sri Lankan had of me all these
years later. I was profoundly ashamed I ever used my memory of
him as an example of anything other than one of the many random acts of kindness happening daily, all around the world. I
was thankful he gave me the perfect ending to a story that shows
we shouldn't forget there is something fundamentally good
about people. Finally, I want to believe that, if given the exact
same circumstances, I would still be trusting enough to accept
help from the fishermen all over again.

Pirates

❦

As far as weather is concerned, the crossing of the Arabian Sea was one of my most beautiful passages ever. The mild-mannered northeast monsoon pushed my little boat and me, wing on wing, over the gentle swells that carried us westward. For twenty-eight days, between Sri Lanka, off the southeastern coast of India, and Djibouti, nestled on the North African side of the entrance to the Red Sea, we chased one beautiful sunrise followed by one spectacular sunset after another. I read, I cooked and I cleaned, thoroughly enjoying the calm postcard perfection as an interlude between the more difficult passages that lay both in our wake and yet to come.

I relished the ideal conditions for all they were worth, knowing full well that, when the pendulum swung, it could go all the way, as it was doing so efficiently with my fears. This idyllic crossing would have contained all the ingredients for a cruising dream if it hadn't been for a nagging undercurrent of worry. This was the ingredient that served as a reminder of the dark side of paradise, the one I had as little control over as the weather. It was the fear of things beyond my control, and in particular, of hostile boats appearing out of nowhere, bearing cutthroat brigands prepared to overwhelm and destroy me.

Statistically, the odds of crossing paths with a pirate are pretty slim, not enough for any real concern except in some completely avoidable pockets on the planet. But, one tragic story of piracy in the Straits of Malacca will have the same debilitating effect on the international cruising community as *Jaws* has had on countless otherwise carefree wave hoppers around the world.

The single most dramatic influence on my frame of mind as I crossed the Arabian Sea was a cruising guide. In those days, it was the only source of information available for sailors in that area, and I read it thoroughly. Every nuance of every description or piece of advice was analyzed from every imaginable angle, taken apart and put back together in a way to fit my current mood and the prevailing conditions. I would obsess over the pictures and charts, and especially over the unchanging words that described what was unknown to me in black and white. I would clutch on to the promise of good as gospel truth and two minutes later, completely blow out of proportion any hint of the bad. When the bad got described as more than a hint, I would be driven to distraction.

On my way to Djibouti, I had to pass the island of Socotra, a rather largish chunk of land off the northeast tip of Somalia that belongs to South Yemen. The most direct route would have hugged the north coast of Socotra, but the cruising guide convinced me of the wisdom of a detour, even if it meant extra mileage and an extra day at sea. Alan Lucas, the author of the *Red Sea and Indian Ocean Cruising Guide*, writes, "Having no useful port and being peopled by a mixture of folk who tend to make their own rules regardless of their government's policy, the visiting yachtsman is warned away. Vessels have been grappled and towed into shore for looting in the past. Under no circumstances find yourself becalmed close in without means of steaming offshore."

In this book full of information, there are only two other references to Socotra. In the section summarizing the hospitableness of regions covered by the book, Lucas says, "Socotra must also be avoided." And, on the next page, under the "Pirates" heading, Socotra earns itself one last mention as Lucas corrects another yachting author's misinformation about piracy in the Red Sea: "In fact, each act of piracy occurred outside the Red Sea, not within, and the name 'Red Sea' was for reference only. The incidents occurred at Socotra and Somalia and anyone venturing to those countries is either misinformed or not informed at all."

He closes all discussion with: "Somalia and Socotra need not be included in this chapter [on piracy] because they are not suggested as places of rest or recreation anywhere in this book." Period. You can't get much clearer warning than that. Socotra. It is a name that still gives me the chills whenever I hear it or see it on a map.

Socotra, Socotra, Socotra. As we got closer to the island's vicinity, Socotra and images of Socotran bandits haunted my dreams and poisoned my waking hours. When the faint purple outline of the island's mountains appeared on the very distant horizon, every whitecap became an approaching boat and I steered even further off course. I don't think I ever got closer than thirty miles offshore, but that still felt way too close. My engine was an unreliable means of steaming anywhere, and the level of my agitation fluctuated with the wind. When it eased enough for the mainsail to begin to flap, I felt ready to jump overboard with a pair of flippers . . . whatever it took to get away from that den of thieves as fast as possible.

I tend to practice avoidance, not confrontation, and before setting off to sail the oceans of the world, this philosophy guided my decisions in preparing myself to counter the piracy threat. A gun was never an option. They repulse me, and I knew that having a gun and not being ready or equipped to use it would be worse than not having anything at all. Plus, I had a hard enough time keeping up with engine maintenance, and in that salty and corrosive atmosphere, there was no way I would have been sufficiently on top of things to have a gun work for me when it was needed. No. Firearms were for Charlton Heston, not me.

Instead, I traveled with an empty hand grenade and a fake

beard. Yup, off the island of Socotra, that was all I had. The theory behind these props was that, to a potential pirate, a grenade-toting, bearded person would be as effective a deterrent as a quivering girl wielding a non-functioning gun. All I had to do was stand on deck, hair and beard whipping about my face in the wind (because there is always wind in my imagination), pull the pin on the grenade and shout, "If you come any closer, I'm taking you all with me (because, in my imagination, everyone understands English)!"

There I was, with the disquieting racket of the mainsail flapping against the shuddering spreaders and the slapping of the waves up under the transom of a boat that wasn't moving very fast, watching each whitecap until it dissipated and each cloud shadow until it moved on. I would look at the beard and grenade on the cockpit bench beside me, and cry in despair wishing I had flame-throwers, bazookas, Rambo on board, and a navy escort. A few minutes later, I'd look at the beard and grenade beside me again and laugh at my fears, semi-aware I was riding a seesaw of emotions intensified by the uncluttered emptiness around me, an emptiness that remained constant. The faint smudge of the mountains in the distance never got any closer and because of the close attention I was paying to the sea around my little universe, instead of menacing craft, I noticed other life-affirming things such as whales, dolphins, jellyfish, and other leaping creatures.

Finally, as all traces of Socotran existence disappeared behind us, I began to realize, yet again, that pirate-related thoughts were part of the package, and they came and went along with a full gamut of other worries and wonders. Without the bad for contrast, how could I appreciate the good? Sunsets were replaced by long dark nights followed by sunrises. Pirates today would be traded in for reefs and enormous amounts of shipping tomorrow. I could have had guns, state of the art navigational equipment, radar detectors, bright lights, and enormous battery banks for insulation from the danger. But then I would have become

dependent on the technology to protect me, and between learning how to use these defenses and maintaining and servicing
them, I wouldn't have had the time to just experience real life,
the whole deal, fears and all.

PART 2

On Board

Barefoot

⁓

Okay, we're all different, and thank God for that, because discoveries of the more absurd differences are what float my boat. Take, for instance, the subject of feet. We can all agree that no two feet are alike, even on the same person. This isn't headline news for anyone. Or is it? I can't even know that for sure because we're all different. But, for the sake of this discussion, let's stick with the idea all feet are different. Linked by a complicated series of body parts, these feet are connected to the host brain, where all the differences get processed, the same brain that decides whether the feet need shoes, or not. Unbelievably, in recent years, I have noticed indignant letters to editors and conversations making this a very divisive choice, that there are people who would like to mandate shoes for everyone on boats. And, even if a foot ends up in my mouth, this is what I'd like to talk about today.

I know, many different brains are now asking the same question: what do feet and footgear have to do with boats? I'll tell you, starting at the beginning. When I was sixteen, I took my first step ever onto the deck of a sailboat, and my first sail ever was a daylong trip from Falmouth to the Scilly Islands, off the English coast. It was a windy, wet, and cold ride, and the memory of my first seasickness ever is accompanied by the smell medley of sloshing bilge water, damp wool, foul-weather gear, and rubber boots on wrinkled feet. From there, the boat headed toward Spain and these blue boots stayed with my feet only until it got warm enough to throw them into the back of the wet locker. Barefoot, I learned how to hold a good course, track ships on the horizon during night watches, do simple navigation, the first lessons I picked up about life on boats. It wasn't until many years later that I discovered I inadvertently chose an ideological stance by getting rid of the boots and joining, not the deck shoe crowd, but the barefoot crowd.

Very little thought went into taking the bare footpath. It happened innocently, as my personal comfort level and preferences developed, and not at all in defiance of the shoe industry of the eighties. Except for several trips in more northern climates where good socks and boots are absolutely vital to toe preservation, I have gone barefoot ever since. Gaining a foothold with flesh pressed to the deck has always felt much safer, and way more comfortable. There have been the exceptional days when, at the hour the sun was at its highest and the decks at their hottest, I've needed to protect the soles of my feet. Otherwise, socks are hard to keep dry, sandals get smelly, deck shoes get salty and stiff, they give me blisters, and all shoes make all decks feel more slippery. As a footnote, it also occurs to me that bare feet are easier to clean and so, decks are cleaner without shoes tracking dinghy scum, sand, and street dirt all over the place. Being of Swiss origin, which usually means an acute sensitivity to cleanliness, I have even come to equate cleanliness with bare feet, and always take off my shoes before boarding a boat.

That I had secured a footing in one camp over another never entered my mind until thirteen years and tens of thousands of miles later, when the time came for me to learn how to teach sailing. Although sailing wasn't rocket science to me, teaching it was a whole different feat, altogether. Knowing how to do something yourself has nothing to do with being able to demonstrate it effectively. If I was going to put my best foot forward in a possible teaching career, this problem needed help.

The solution was located in Key West where Captain Carol and the domestic program of the sailing school that hired me were based. Carol was a veteran of many years of instruction and I taught under her for four days. On the first day, as soon as everyone had introduced herself, Carol began with a lesson on shipboard rules, rudimentary nautical vocabulary, and safety guidelines. I listened and took notes on her delivery, admiring the clarity and focused authority of her speech, until she said something that got my toes tingling.

"Look at this deck and all the potential hazards," she said. "You must protect your feet at all times with a good pair of shoes." She pointed to her deck shoes as an example of acceptable non-skidding, non-marking footwear. I looked down at my bare feet and sat on them. What she said made sense, I thought, but we were talking about an ingrained practice here. I didn't even own a pair of boat shoes and all they sell in places like Key West are platforms. I had a private talk with Carol later, and she reassured me that she was as footloose as one can get; she knew I could take care of my own toes. In fact, Carol really didn't care about other people's feet until she became responsible for teaching toes unfamiliar with deck layouts how to avoid blood and pain, hence her captain's edict.

Ever since, though, I've noticed how individuals will come down heavily on either side of the debate. They wonder aloud, and in print, about the peril of playing footsie with deck tackle, but for me, this risk hasn't proved itself to be any worse on a deck than what it has been with doorsills, chair legs, Lego pieces, and tree roots, worldwide. I've done some fancy footwork, hopping around a cockpit, whining and cursing over a throbbing digit, as often as I have anywhere else below deck, and in other places nowhere near a boat. This just happens to be one of life's hazards, almost as dangerous, I think, as getting out of bed every morning, especially if there are any footstools or footlockers nearby.

I've also begun to pay more attention to who will and who

won't wear shoes on a boat in the tropics, which has led me, footsore, to several conclusions, based, of course, on some pretty wide generalities. Charter guests and day sailors will wear shoes; cruisers and live-aboards won't. Older and wiser people will; younger and more reckless people won't. People who prefer towns will; those who prefer small villages and remote anchorages won't. Northerners will; southerners won't. Clean-cut people in khakis and polo shirts will; long-haired types with body piercings and tattoos won't.

Finally, there are the people who think there is a right or wrong answer to the shoe question, and there are those who don't. As for my footstone on the subject, there is only one footle left to say: As long as the shoes fit, we can each decide if we want to wear them, or not.

Swimming

After a spell of dismal January weather, last week we were given a glorious day of bright blue skies with temperatures hovering pleasantly near the freezing point. The fields and forest around the house were crisp and white with snow. Inspired to venture outside, I donned my knee-high snow boots and without a second thought, set off up the hill to visit my neighbor. At the halfway point, the steepest section of the woods, I stopped, heaving great gulps of air, realizing I had seriously underestimated the depth of the snow. Once again, my eyes were bigger than my brain. Instead of several inches, every step sunk me down to well over my knees, progress was exhaustingly slow, and I just wanted to give up. But I couldn't. I'm not a quitter for that kind of thing. Instead, I focused on putting one foot in front of the other enough times to reach Kathy's house, her wood stove, a cup of hot tea, and a pair of snow shoes for the return.

This over-ambitious hike reminded me of the many occasions I have impulsively decided to swim out to a boat, or to land, only to have the fun part end somewhere around the midway point, where I found myself asking a familiar question: Why do I do this to myself? I think this is something we all can relate to: experiences that may start out as good ideas until suddenly, they become ordeals, no longer adventures, no matter the attitude. Whatever the circumstances, we've all been there, and the adventure part only comes when it's over, when there's a story to tell.

The connection between a nightmare slog in the snow and other previous long distance swimming fiascoes made me think about a surprisingly common confession. I can't even begin to count the times I've heard that not knowing how to swim became a major impediment to taking on sailing as a hobby, vacation, or lifestyle. "There is nothing I'd like to do more than learn how to sail," it has been said, "but I can't swim!"

Now, these words don't come from the mouths of desert dwellers for whom water in any large quantity is as fearsome and alien as the desert can be to those who haven't made it home for centuries. They come from people attending boat shows, sailing seminars, and schools, and I have something to say about this.

Since the age of five, I've been a very good doggie paddler and can still remember the day I first discovered how instinctive this elementary stroke can be in the event of involuntary submersion. My younger sisters, brother, and I were horsing around a poolside on the Jersey shore when my father suddenly picked me up and threw me in the deep end. Aside from being introduced to the concept of betrayal, it must not have been too traumatic an experience because all I remember is a terrible fright, and how, from then on, the doggie paddle became second nature. Over the years, it slowly evolved into a passable breaststroke and nothing more, nothing less, which is all anyone ever needs on a boat.

The sailing environment is very conducive to swimming-related diversions, especially in turquoise, reef-strewn destinations where an underwater world waiting to be discovered beckons. Or, when the weather in the tropical belt dominated by most of the sailing culture gets so hot frequent dips become the only relief available. Or, when the keel needs a scrubbing, or when the propeller finds a rope or lobster pot. There are times when a modest swimming ability will come in handy and I've always managed to get by with my hybrid doggie-paddle-breaststroke.

Considering humans and planet Earth, itself, are made up of more than seventy-percent water, it's pretty amazing we all don't swim before we walk. My sister, the one who knows everything and pulls facts out of a bottomless hat, told me people aren't afraid of snakes or water upon birth. It is only once we hear the snake and water stories, she says, once we are exposed to fear, that we deny our primal instincts and make room for the dread to take root and mature. If we don't learn how to swim as a child, before the phobias have become too ingrained, I believe the challenge becomes more daunting, but not impossible.

It's like taking on skiing, or swing dancing, or the piano, at any point beyond adolescence. Some things just don't get any easier to pick up with age, especially once we've been introduced to fright or embarrassment; unlearning fear is much harder to do than to learn the actual thing we fear. If only my father had also pushed me down a mountain on skis. I've sailed around the world by myself but nowadays, I can only perform timid switchbacks behind my kamikaze seven year old who tears down black diamond slopes. I started to ski two years ago with him and already, he has eclipsed my over-cautious and clumsy efforts. And, forget about dancing!

At least I've learned how to get down the slopes in one piece and I'd like to take this opportunity to stress to anyone who might be thinking of swimming lessons how incredibly unimportant it is to be able to swim like a Greg Louganis before getting on a boat. Sure, master the basics, but don't go overboard.

Another fact I remember hearing or reading somewhere is that old time sailors never knew how to swim; it would have brought bad luck because unless one is extremely troubled, nobody jumps overboard on purpose. Usually, men overboard are accidents that take place at inconvenient moments, such as in the middle of the ocean, the night, or a storm, where the Olympic swimmer without some flotation device will end up in as hopeless a predicament as the non-swimmer.

The ticket is in putting more energy into overboard prevention tactics. As far as skill goes, once Doggie Paddle 101 has been mastered, you're on your way. And to avoid the predicament

I found myself in on the snowy hill last week, don't plan on swimming the English Channel if you are only good for half the distance because, trust me, the second half won't be much fun.

Overboard

Aboard a boat I once skippered on a tour of the Greek Islands, one of the guests was a shaman from the south. Her power animal was the wolf and, normally, she ran with some other wolfish types in New England. But to join this cruise she had split temporarily with the pack. She tended to function on a plane where people like to frolic about in the buff while speaking of the universal powers that bring us all together, and the rest of us found her amusing.

On one windless, unclothed-for-her afternoon, midway between Paros and Mykonos, just as she was telling me about a past life as Joan of Arc's mother, I looked over her shoulder and saw a big fluke slice through the glassy water off our bow. "Something big ahoy!" I shouted.

Books were dropped and everyone clambered to the lifeline as I cut the engine and we drifted up alongside a massive manta ray. The wingspan must have been a good six feet, (maybe more, but my memory prefers to under-guess) and cameras were whipped out as the cluster excitedly watched the beautiful creature gracefully skim the surface. All eyes but one pair were on the manta.

The shaman was looking at me instead, drawling, "Stop the boat, oh, please stop the boat. I have to swim with this magnificence."

I hesitated before reversing the engine as she belly flopped into the Mediterranean. The idea of people jumping off boats without awaiting docks or dinghies always makes me a little nervous. It makes me hear warning voices in my head, kind of like the ones Joan of Arc used to hear before they tied her to a burning stake. As it turned out, the shaman was an under-appreciated intrusion into the manta's world. With a single stroke of its muscled wings, it plunged out of sight before we had time to attach the boarding ladder for the sea nymph, who was disappointed she hadn't been offered a piggy back ride over the cerulean sea.

On yet another becalmed afternoon off the Balearic Islands in the western Mediterranean, during a cockpit game of hearts with a different crew, an enormous loggerhead sea turtle fell in love with our hull. Again, cards and books were dropped and everyone hung over the lifelines, watching the hard shell belly up with the swell and knock against us, over and over again, its reptilian eyes gazing adoringly at the hunk of fiberglass keel. I was relieved that nobody wanted to jump in this time. This whole group preferred appreciating the world below us from the deck above it, as much as the shaman might have enjoyed jumping in to rub snouts with the turtle.

I've got to say the last thing I ever want to do is jump in the water to mingle with sea life. If I read about a man swimming in dark offshore waters with barracudas, sharks, or a beluga whale, it gives me the willies. When somebody climbs back aboard with a story of a moray eel sighting, the deck feels even more reassuring. I prefer being a member of the ship or shore-bound audience. I'm only human, by definition a surface mammal. For me, if it's too deep to see the bottom, swimming is reserved for emergencies, when duty calls to cut a line away from a shaft, or to check the hull for damage from a rock encounter.

It wasn't always like this. I shudder at the memory of my naïve sixteen-year-old body being trolled for fun behind a boat in the middle of the Atlantic. Or, then watching my little sister, whom I love, put on her harness and dive overboard at the end of the line, surfing down one wave after another at minnow speed. I'm glad we survived, that I did it, but I'll never again make like a piece of bait and jump into the deep ocean for pleasure.

I'll call to sharks, dolphins, whales, and turtles from the cockpit and bow pulpit, but I don't think for a second that we speak the same language, and it's okay. They have their world below the water, I have mine above it, and I am grateful when they make themselves known, because it doesn't happen so often anymore. The ray manta and turtle were exceptions. In the past ten years, for every trip with a sighting, I've been on another trip without seeing any fish except trophies mounted on yacht club walls. My friend John, who has been sailing small sailboats in coastal and offshore waters full time for a quarter of a century, has noticed the change, too. "The ocean is dying," he says. "I see fewer and fewer signs of life."

Even so, when I hang off the stern for an offshore cool down, I think about the guy who pulled himself up the boarding ladder of another boat I was on, seconds before a sixteen-foot shark swooped up from the mid-Atlantic depths. I'll keep looking over my shoulders for shadows lurking behind heads of brain coral, never forgetting a Red Sea anchorage, a shark swimming past me, and me frantically paddling right back to the safety of my boat.

I'm not alone and if you're with me on this one, I'd like to say, for the record, there's nothing wrong with submersion avoidance. It's instinctive. I'll go a step further and say a fear of the sea and what lies beneath, as long as there is still something alive there to fear—and not just toxic waste, unexploded depth charges, and ordnance dumping grounds—is perfectly healthy. Old time sailors never even learned how to swim because there was only one reason to end up in the water, and that happened when knowing how to swim would just prolong the inevitable end.

Waves can come crashing over the bow, surging under the

stern, and as long as there is gravity, air, and a bow and stern underfoot to talk about, I'm fine. Fundamentally, I believe we're not water animals, even if some of us are more in touch with our inner fish. I'm not. If you are, though, go ahead, dive in. By all means enjoy it, love it, but just know that I won't be able to relax until you're back on board again, where I'll be waiting.

Kitchens

Many sailing memories resurface periodically to remind me of another life parallel to my current one in Vermont, with its fair share of weather, lawn mower and car engine related problems, natural beauty, and the kitchen. Interestingly, many are snippets of companionship, smells and sounds, of meals and mealtimes spent around the galley and saloon, preparing, serving, and eating food.

Comparing the history of mankind to the history of cruising, a way of life that started pretty much with Joshua Slocum barely 100 years ago, reveals the modern sailor as embryonic. Still, humans have come a long way in what is now believed to be 3.5 million years, and in all that time, one thing hasn't changed: we still need to eat. Ever since Prometheus stole fire from Zeus for us mortals, the home fires have been burning and we've been hanging out around the hearth. How often do hosts or hostesses succeed in herding guests into a living or dining room? The main cluster of every gathering always prefers the kitchen, close to the food and cook, the fridge, the stove, the drinks, the good smells; all these together add up to comfort, and at all levels, comfort is number one.

There are many different kinds of cruising boats and comfort levels, but almost without exception, galleys and saloons are adjacent, separated by cupboards, engine rooms, bulkheads, railings, or steps, anything convenient for wedging in the cook in conditions ranging from gentle beats to wicked storms (in case anyone still feels like cooking). Lives revolve around feeding schedules, gourmet or not, and whether we are harbor, island, or ocean hopping, the kerosene, alcohol, or gas one-burner or two-burner stove, and the oven are the center of the sailing halo, essential to happiness.

Together, the galley and saloon symbolize the universal hearth, adapted to the boating environment, a system reliant upon good stowage skills, cubbyholes, sliding doors, drawers, shelving and cabinets that also contain seacocks, pumps, plumbing and wiring. Too many cooks spoil the broth, provision redundantly, have different organizing techniques, and for things to run smoothly, there usually is a head chef, the captain of the kitchen, a title in no way inferior to being in charge of navigation, the proper management of which is also essential to happiness.

I am capable of filling both positions, but I have to say my preference resides with the galley. If necessary, I can figure out an engine or rigging repair, how to anchor to code, when to efficiently reef, dock, tack and run, how to get through all that can happen in the world beyond the kitchen I keep returning to because, on land or at sea, the kitchen is my second favorite place. My first favorite is a bed, or bunk, anywhere I can sleep off all the kitchen work.

One of the most vivid galley memories from my days of sailing the big oceans concerns a storm. This storm had it all: the mountainous waves, the howling winds, the crashing and pounding of 25,000 pounds of fiberglass sailing off thirty-foot-high walls of raging liquid. On my father's boat, with three other frightened and sick guys, I spent two days in the cockpit, huddled under the dodger, lashed in above the sliding companionway hatch. Sometimes, I'd make it to the vicinity of overboard for hygienic reasons, the only reason good enough for me to leave the somewhat sheltered spot where I slept, fantasizing about my happy place, or despairingly watched the heaving mountains, waiting for the final blow.

Toward the end of my first true tempest, two of our crew got ferried away by a nearby Coast Guard cutter out rescuing another boat. Hours after they left, the winds and swells began to die, and slowly my father, the remaining friend, and I reclaimed our happiness. I crawled below to clean up the kitchen because, at the age of seventeen, I already knew the galley well. I knew where to find the extra sponges, soap, buckets, and garbage. Before starting the cleanup, I first made a cup of tea—a steaming, hot cup of tea with a spoon of sugar and a cloud of milk. After days of heaving, forcing some water down only because you're supposed to, and popping the occasional Dramamine out of desperation, nothing ever had, or has ever since tasted so good. A couple of hours later, we caught a beautiful bluefish and fried it up in butter. Heaven.

A storm may be a period of intense suffering and misery, followed by sheer exultation when we survive to tell the tale and my tale wouldn't be complete without the hearth, this one unforgettably delicious cup of tea, and the meal that followed. Surrounded by the comforting ambience of food and drink, the three of us sat around the table in the saloon, crafting a new life for the storm into the story we still tell seventeen years later.

Christmas

It's here again, that time of year between Thanksgiving and Boxing Day, and in the spirit of the season, I just visited my shelf of reference books full of nautical lore and anecdotes to see if Christmas and the ocean have ever been historically connected. Book after book, I found nothing, not a single mention of the holiday. Two thousand years of nautical history and celebrating Christmas have never come together in a way significant enough to merit mention. Amazing.

Frustrated, I then spied the logbook from my years aboard VARUNA on the same shelf, its slender black binding nearly hidden by the hefty tomes surrounding it. Aha! What was I thinking? Fourteen years ago, alone with my cat, I spent Christmas in the doldrums belt of the Indian Ocean, an expanse of water on either side of the equator. This mote of a book turned out to have more seasonally relevant information than any whale of a reference book, a personalized connection between Christmas and the sea, and my very own history to rewrite.

The cover of the logbook is creased and well worn, the pages filled with the words and drawings that articulate and illustrate every mood a girl is capable of experiencing between eighteen and twenty-one. This may be an emotionally volatile part of life under normal circumstances, but when Christmas and being alone on the ocean are thrown into the mix . . . let's just say it was a good thing I was alone.

Here is my first entry on that day: *"December 25, 1986. 07:23. Compass Course 360°. Speed 4 knots. Stopped the boat for a while. Seems as though the wind may have veered. We'll see. Opened my presents—one beautiful feather earring and a necklace that Olivier* [my boyfriend and future husband] *made. I wonder if he opened mine yet, and if he likes them* [I think I gave him chocolates and whiskey]. *I am in a rather bad mood, screaming at Tarzoon* [my cat, poor thing]. *It is Christmas Day, a huge squall is overtaking us and there is at least one more week left before land, probably more. New Year will also be spent at sea. Opened a can of miniature hot-dogs and plan to mix them with ham, sauerkraut, and potatoes."*

Our last landfall, coincidentally, had been Christmas Island, a speck in the southern Indian Ocean west of Australia some explorer with a creative propensity for naming new lands must have discovered on Christmas Day. We were headed for Sri Lanka which was once named Serendib, hence the word "serendipity."

With hundreds of miles behind and ahead of us, I can't read many Christmas-like or serendipitous feelings in between the lines. Who would if they were looking forward to a pressure-cooked meal of sauerkraut and canned meat of uncertain origin?

Being in the middle of the Indian Ocean for Christmas, I felt pretty sorry for myself, imagining my family gathered around a decorated, real, and prickly Christmas tree, probably talking about me. Even if there weren't any snow outside, they would still be dressed in the turtlenecks and other wintry outfits I was missing just because wearing them would have meant I wasn't roasting alone on the equator.

Later that day, I wrote in my log book: *"12:19. Stopped the boat, sails slamming very annoyingly. Please let me have a nice wind! Happy Christmas, Olivier. It would be so nice if we could be together. Reading* Clan of the Cave Bear. *Had tomato juice and ham. No turkey, no eggnog."*

I could see my siblings having a moment of silence for me, just before gulping down the eggnog. Would they fast, or have some canned ravioli in solidarity with me? No. Perhaps they would talk briefly about what I was eating as they cut into a turkey, or rosemary-encrusted roast pork. They might feel a fleeting pang of regret for not having sent me anything as they tore wrapping paper away from a pile of gifts. They might think out there on the balmy, shining sea, I wouldn't need the new sweaters, gloves and socks they were receiving. Oh, lucky me. What did they know?

On the upper left hand corner of this page in the log book, there is a list of dates and locations: *1986 Indian Ocean, 1985 Tahiti and New York, 1984 New York, 1983 Guadeloupe.* I was revisiting three Christmases prior to this one, remembering and comparing the differences. In 1985, I had flown home from Tahiti to New York to see my mother for the last time before she died. In 1984, I was in New York, unwrapping charts, short wave radios, and all sorts of other stuff in anticipation of my upcoming voyage. In 1983, my father, friend Fritz, my sister, and I made it to Guadeloupe after an Atlantic crossing just in time to go out for a Christmas dinner. Several days before making our landfall, we had crossed wakes with another sailboat from Ireland with a decorated Christmas tree hanging from the backstay.

On the Indian Ocean, though, far from any major shipping lanes, my chances of running into another boat were pretty slim. No matter how this pudding was cut, I was wassailing alone. On the upper right hand corner of the page, I kept a list of books read, and two books down after *The Clan of the Cave Bear* I see *One Hundred Years of Solitude.*

My last log entry of the day says: *"20:55. Compass Course 340°. Speed 4-5 knots. Wind coming from NE. Put up sails and we're beating into it. Don't know if it's just another squall or real wind* [according to following entries, the wind had come to stay, brisk and from the north, a headwind, which is kind of like a lump of coal in the stocking]. *The batten broke again, I fixed it again. Made the sauerkraut. It was very good. Gave Tarzoon ham, but he doesn't like it. Well, Christmas is over—next occasion, New Year . . ."*

And so my entry for the day tapers off. As I write now, and

notice every detail of this page from my life, I am able to relive the agony I felt out there, separated from everyone I loved. The watermarks smearing the black pen are obviously from teardrops and I'm sure my loneliness was heartfelt, but no matter how hard I try, I can't rekindle that self-pity. No way. I have everything I wished for then—companionship, children, a house, a garden, and roots. What I didn't know then, as a twenty year old on her own boat, was that I would catch up with the future, and that this day would be a gift to treasure as one Christmas to remember for the rest of my life.

Never again would my concerns be so basic and essential, worrying about flat calms, slow progress, broken engines, torn sails, leaking chainplates and climbing the mast to replace a dead bulb. Instead, I'd be making lists, worrying about time passing too quickly, budgets, rising prices, and feeling manipulated by the commercialism that is equated with a Merry Christmas. Staring at flapping sail and wishing for a steady wind, I couldn't see far enough beyond the bow pulpit to trust that the wind always comes back. One year flows into the next, and the simplicity of this day stands apart in my memory now, sharply and in a context that no reference book, or all the other Christmases, before and since 1986, could hold a flaming Yule log to.

Overkill

⁓

Simplicity just doesn't seem to be cool these days. We talk about the environment, global warming, rising ocean temperatures, over-fishing, over-eating, over-killing, and we still keep over-consuming. This need for more, bigger, better, and faster has come at the expense of many things, including common sense. Even the sailing culture can't escape the inventors who are part of an economy that requires growth, where honoring the capacity for basic human ability becomes a threat to the wallet. Industry magazines, catalogs, and boat shows are full of gimcrack and geegaw landfillers, mostly dispensable stuff that sailors have managed to survive without for centuries.

Compared to life ashore, cruising is a simpler way to go, mainly by virtue of the size of the living arrangements available on a boat. No matter the length or width, a boat will never have as many walk-in closets and empty garage space as a five-thousand-square-foot house. When one gets on a boat for any extended period of time, sacrifices on some level must be made. Few people realize how little we need until they actually live with little and learn to wonder at how others could need so much. But, within this sub-culture of simplicity, the differences on the scale of needs fluctuate like the stock market (which wouldn't survive if our needs weren't being manufactured along with the products meant to satisfy them).

I could use many examples of marketing strategies that make

us feel guilty for depriving ourselves of the latest whatnot, but my pet peeve is with navigation equipment. The electronic age has caught up to the cruiser with a vengeance. It is entirely possible to interface weather faxes, radars, chart programs, radios, Autohelms, telephones, fax machines, depth sounders, global positioning systems, and things I haven't even heard of, to each other so that a boat could feasibly make a remote controlled passage. This is a triumph of technology over humanity, an electronic age that is doing its best to convince us we are too stupid and physically weak to do what it can do for us, at a price. I once sailed a boat across the Atlantic and we didn't even have to leave the cockpit to raise the sails—it all happened at the push of a button.

Before boarding this new boat in France to bring it to Baltimore, my last voyage had been the same crossing on my 26-foot boat with a sextant, an electronic watch, tables, a depth sounder, a VHF radio, a mechanical self-steering apparatus, a compass, and an EPIRB that may or may not have worked. Some may say that I was woefully and irresponsibly under-equipped—and they have—and it's true there was many a time I wished I had a slightly larger boat, a radar, a SatNav, something to lessen the work-and-worry load, but in the end, I was all the more prouder for having done the trip with the little support I had. Not only was it much simpler not to rely upon technology, but I also learned one could manage very well without it.

So, when I stepped aboard the new boat in the French yard to live the alternative, I was blown away. The owner had ordered every single extra from the manufacturer and what the French couldn't provide, he shipped over from the States. This was over ten years ago and a lot of new things have been invented since, but back then, this was as outfitted a boat as I had ever seen. Every imaginable navigational or safety device on the market had been installed or stored in lockers. We had bells, whistles, and horns, wet suits and dry suits, life rafts, watermakers, life vests, harnesses and harness-life vest combinations, an EPIRB the size of R2D2, an owner and three licensed captains, including myself (my husband was head-captain). This is just the list of things I remember. I also remember being put off by the excess and feeling fidgety about all the attention paid to potential disaster that could very well have become a self-fulfilling prophecy.

We set sail and stopped in Spain and the Azores, pushing buttons, reading digital displays, and poring over the squiggly lines on weather faxes which were great for extending the period of nervous anticipation before the gales hit. On each and every watch, in flat calm or blow, the owner lashed himself behind the wheel. He checked and double-checked all his safety equipment and the backups. He worried incessantly with an air of affected nonchalance, I was pregnant and moody, and everything about the trip began to irritate me.

Then, one day, in the middle of the ocean, somewhere between the Azores and the Chesapeake, we found ourselves becalmed and the owner decided he wanted to have a mid-ocean swim experience for the scrapbook. I've jumped overboard in very deep and calm water in my lifetime, but I don't do it anymore because I've also seen big predatory animals and don't fancy the idea of becoming bait. I like feeling the security of the deck underfoot and long ago passed the age where the thrill of kicking my legs above God-knows-what is exciting. Instead, I sat on the cockpit coaming and watched the owner.

He dove off the bow, paddled to the stern, clambered back on board, and with a beaming smile, shook himself off like a puppy and declared he wanted to do it again. So he did. For the second time, he jumped off the bow, headed for the stern, and pulled himself up on the ladder. It was an experience identical to the first, only this time, a matter of seconds after his last dripping toe left the water, a sixteen-foot shark swooped up from the depths in the same spot, swerving and grazing alongside the hull before leaving.

The poor fellow turned sheet-white and was shaking like a

leaf. For a moment, the rest of us were concerned he was having a heart attack. Who wouldn't after coming so close to losing major body parts? When he recovered, it was my turn to suffer from the decorum that prevented me from pointing out the obvious irony in the situation. As sophisticated and outfitted as he had made his boat, no amount of money could have prevented an encounter with that shark. Luck and wits are still human commodities no gadget can replace. We have to make comfort level decisions on our own and not let an industry that needs to eat and fill its walk-in closets influence us otherwise. Our wallets and the richness of our own experiences will be much better off if we can remember this when we prepare for the unknown.

Simplicity

I'm starting to sound old, but things just aren't the way they used to be. I, and anyone who bothers to listen, can hear it in what I catch myself saying, especially about modernity, and to what extent gadgetry replaces good old-fashioned work and self-reliance. My ex-mother in law had a tendency to go on about the unnecessary introduction of dishwashers into a world that survived well enough without them for thousands of years. "What does anybody need one for?" she'd ask, while scrubbing a pot. "Look, this sink full of hot water and a steel wool pad work just as well, faster, and make less noise." Her points were inarguable. Since her son was raised to scorn them, I didn't have a dishwasher either, and I was inclined to agree.

Convenience is the only point to be made in favor of a dishwasher, or any of the other things I rail against in a stubbornly Luddite and broken LP-record way. More conveniences, I keep insisting, still aren't buying us time to enjoy a simpler quality of life. They just end up making us think we always need more deadweight, complicating things further and insulating us from our own self-accountability. What's scary is that my mother-in-law is actually over seventy years old, while I only sound that way as I continue to swim upstream behind her, fighting the raging current.

I get the marine industry catalogs, I read the articles about all the stuff people keep installing on boats, and I know the whole cruising lifestyle has evolved considerably in terms of equipment since the days when I was living aboard. But, that wasn't so long ago, relatively speaking. The late eighties aren't yet considered the dark ages of technology in the big picture, and I'm not a graybeard either. But, when you start analyzing the details of the small pictures, the way the average cruising boat was outfitted then, and the way it tends to be geared up now, it is like choosing between a four-cylinder Yugo and an eight-cylinder SUV. For some people, four cylinders are enough.

I've been doing a lot of chartering with the cheaper companies, where the height of sophistication means a CD player and an electrical windlass that works. Because of the nature of their calling, charter boats don't go very crazy in the gear department, as this is also the arena for most failures. The last thing a charterer with ten days wants to do is spend five days figuring out and fixing systems; the last thing a charter company wants to do is chase down a broken boat in some faraway anchorage to make the repairs themselves. So, they minimize conveniences and go with tried and true basics, which always works for me. As long as the standard engine, rigging, and ground tackle are in order, the VHF radio works and there are enough charts and a good pilot book to cover the area in which we are sailing, I am happy. Throw in buttons, lights, alarms, and interfaced doohickeys to control any of these functions with all their potential for failure, and I become a nervous wreck with anxiety dreams. For me, the key to feeling confidently comfortable on a boat, and most anywhere else, is, and has been always, simplicity.

Let me take you on a trip down memory lane, back to the 26-foot Contessa I called home for two-and-a-half years, the boat that got me around the world. VARUNA was just about as simple as they get, as simple as the rationale behind such simplicity. I was only eighteen years old, a girl who never really took apart engines, built models, or showed much interest in engineering or mechanics, but I was handy and smart enough to figure out gears and block and tackle. The rigging amounted to halyards, sheets, lines, blocks and cleats. The ground tackle was rode, chain and a windlass (which broke early on into the trip, so I always hauled it in by hand). I came to understand diesel engines because my one-cylinder, 7.5 horsepower engine often did not work. The galley was a two-burner kerosene stove, and all steering was done with a Monitor self-steering device. My navigation equipment was charts, books, a sextant, a depth sounder, a VHF, an RDF, and a shortwave radio. That's all. I remember looking around VARUNA's cozy interior and feeling I could solve almost any problem, and being content with the straightforwardness.

Many boats were like mine; some had less, some had more. But compared to nowadays, those sailors were purists who relied on sextants, the skies, and a universal time tick as a primary source of positioning, or as backup, instead of owning three GPS units. Prior to Desert Storm, the GPS was available only for military use, and SatNavs were often on the blink, so a good place to get together and talk about the best times for sun sights was around the spigot where we filled jerry cans to haul water back to the boats, where it got rationed according to how much one liked to worry about getting more. Salt water for bathing and doing dishes was fine (in cleaner harbors and definitely at sea); fresh water was for rinsing and cooking (anywhere). With limited tank reserves and no water-makers, we had few freshwater showers.

Reliable refrigeration was sketchy; block-ice, non-perishables, and good long-term provisioning were dependable. Very few boats had televisions and entertainment came in the form of books, listening to the radio, or manufacturing fun with things like hiking, swimming, snorkeling, fishing, fixing stuff, or playing games the old fashioned way, with each other, or Solitaire, if like myself you were alone. Above all, resourcefulness and independence from the conveniences of land-based needs were valued and respected, not disadvantages, but a spice of life.

A few particularly Spartan sailors stick out in my memory.

Olivier, the man I later married, didn't even have a VHF, or electrical navigation lights. Instead, he had red and green kerosene storm lanterns to hang in the rigging. And yet, with just the sextant, he sailed his 32-foot functional, steel ketch to the remotest atolls and islands where no other boats cared to venture and he could fix almost anything without professional help.

Michel, another French character, sailed his 22-foot, glassed-over plywood, and somewhat less functional, daysailer across the Atlantic and the Pacific Oceans, from Africa to Vanuatu, where I met him. He had no VHF or navigation lights, just a lot of chutzpah. Michel, Olivier, and a few others were extremes I could look at and say, "Wow! These guys are doing it with even less than I have."

When I felt sorry for myself, their stories provided another refreshing perspective on how lucky I was to be learning that it is possible to live with less in a world that keeps convincing us we need more.

On a recent trip to New Zealand, I was invited aboard the other extreme. It was about 39-foot-long and it is enough to say this boat was more of a SUV than my Yugo house, with multiple computers, a ham radio for Internet access, a microwave, two VCRs, a watermaker, power tools, a freezer, a generator and inverters, and an electrical Autohelm instead of any mechanical self-steering device.

The boat was a floating luxury condominium, so connected to the world from which it was trying to distance itself. With its fully integrated electronic navigation chart system, I felt as if cruising long distances in out-of-the-way places would be impossible for anyone but a computer savvy electrical engineer. The reliance on so many different systems was oppressive and intimidating, as alien a concept to me as a dishwasher is to my mother-in-law.

Several days later, in another anchorage, a different boat ghosted in under sail and anchored just ahead of us. It was about 34-foot-long, and I gratefully recognized the Monitor self-steering gear attached to the stern. One of our people visited them and returned with the news that here were some cruisers who still used paper charts, knew how to and enjoyed doing celestial navigation, were surviving with saltwater bathing, and didn't need to stick around and get a job to fix or upgrade anything. And, they were perfectly content. I wonder if, when they return to a life ashore, these guys will get a dishwasher. Maybe I should have gone over to ask them. Maybe they would have understood.

Superstition

Superstition is a funny thing. Just about every culture or way of life has some kind of superstitious element and sailors are no exception. We have boatloads of illogical dos and don'ts that provide parameters for some and amusement for others, from refusing to change the name of a second-hand boat, to tattooing open eyes onto eyelids to keep watch while sleeping.

Somewhere deep within even the most cynical among us lurks a kernel of superstitious nature. Almost every sailor will baptize a new boat with a bottle of wine or champagne cracked on the bow, and most sailors own some kind of good luck charm, be it a figurehead of a naked lady, or a coin placed under the mast, a crystal swinging from a string, or some kind of personal item that just feels comforting to have around.

One commonly known superstition dictates a voyage should never begin on a Friday. This rule of the seaway has been affecting sailing itineraries for two thousand years. One origin theory claims it has something to do with the unhappy day on which Jesus was crucified. Whenever it started, at some point in the nineteenth century, a group in the British Navy, perhaps a bunch of annoyed atheists, tried to get rid of the bothersome Friday problem. They laid the keel of a new ship on a Friday, named her the H.M.S. *Friday*, launched her on a Friday, and her maiden voyage began on a Saturday. Or rather, it should have, because she left a day earlier to prove some useless point and was never heard from again.

The first time I purposely left on a Friday, it wasn't to thumb my nose at superstition, but to avoid yet another delay. On the subsequent South Pacific passage, I ran into a storm that could have been avoided had I waited that extra day, the trade winds were unpleasantly rambunctious, the seas were rough, my two cats never used their kitty litter, I fell and sprained my wrist, a bottle of bright red grenadine syrup exploded all over the cabin, I found lice living on my head, and on the last day before landfall, a rotten egg cracked in the food hammock swinging above my bunk. That was enough. I blamed all my woes on the Friday departure and swore my sailing life would never again be inflexible enough to not wait a day.

Soon after that trip, though, I met a Swiss-Frenchman who laughed when I refused to leave on a Friday. He said I was being ridiculous, ignorant, which would have been hard to argue if he didn't get all bent out of shape every time the subject of rabbits came up. Apparently, in the old days, French sailors would throw live rabbits into the holds as underway protein supplements, and while awaiting the wrong end of the dinner table, the critters would gnaw away at lines and timbers, sometimes to disastrous ends, effectively turning modern French sailors into rabbit-phobes who leave the word *rabbit* ashore. So, I laughed right back at this Frenchman and kept an eye out for a rabbit foot on a key chain—just for him.

Because of his teasing, though, one year after the first bad Friday experience, I did it again. I left the Suez Canal, bound for Malta on a Friday. That night, my boat was hit by a ship. Coincidence? I think not. You don't have to bonk me over the head to drive this kind of message home. You get what you ask for. I survived that encounter and spent the next fifteen years successfully dodging Friday departures and finding other things like weather, equipment, and myself to blame arising problems on.

Then, recently I planned a ten-day sailing trip in Greece by looking at dates rather than the days, unwittingly making our first day out a Friday. When I first realized this grievous error several days before we cast off, my heart sank. I immediately found an evil eye and glommed onto it. In Greece, and other countries to the east, to ward off trouble, evil eyes are placed over babies, from taxi rear view mirrors, above doorways, engine rooms, and cattle. I own many of these blue glass baubles because they're cool looking, and they make great last-minute gifts and Christmas tree ornaments. Now, I also needed some of the alleged magic.

The Friday afternoon we left was a beautiful one spent motoring on the calm waters off the coast of mainland Greece, en route from Athens to the island of Kea. Halfway there, we were nearing Cape Sounion where the Temple of Poseidon presides and the eight people in our group were sitting in the cockpit, eating pistachios, trying to figure out the relationships between the gods of the Greek pantheon. I was anxiously waiting to see Poseidon's domain because I had a wine offering to make to the sea god to further appease the fates. Ten miles from the temple, the charter boat engine's rumble turned into a sputter . . . then total silence. I knew it! It was the beginning of the end. Evidently, my pocket-size evil eye wasn't up to the job, and in all the ensuing troubleshooting confusion, I forgot all about Poseidon's offering.

Ten days later, this trip saw the filters fill hourly with water from the contaminated fuel tanks, the blowing out of the exhaust, broken bilge pumps, failing heads, hatches and portholes that leaked in bucketfuls, and lots of pounding through huge waves and howling winds. I couldn't keep my sense of reason from being washed overboard. Of course, things would have turned out very differently had we not left on a Friday.

So, laugh at this poor ignorant fool if you must, you purveyors of cold and scientific reason. But, heed my words when you plan your next trip: there are seven days in a week, six other choices besides Friday. And, if sailing isn't about being flexible with time, learning from mistakes, and respecting things we can't always rationalize, then I'll eat a rabbit's foot.

Water

I just spent ten days cruising the Grenadines on a 51-foot boat with nine ladies and 300 gallons of water at the tail end of the dry season when the islands are brown and scorched. At the chart briefing prior to the trip, the charter company guy told us there would be only two places to get water once we left St. Vincent. We could fill up in Union Island and maybe in Petite Martinique, if they had rebuilt the dock damaged by Hurricane Lenny. He wasn't sure about that, but he did know wherever the topping off would happen, it would cost at least 25 cents the gallon, or 75 dollars for a refill.

Seventy-five dollars for water! "Holy cheapskates!" I thought. That could pay for several really nice meals, a good pair of shoes, or five tanks of gas for my car at home, that is, if we ever needed to take on more water. The ladies on my boat had come to experience and learn something about cruising from me and here, by gum, was incentive for the perfect lesson.

Early in my sailing career, I had learned about water conservation from a severe and, some might say, an overly obsessive teacher. This was my father. In the early eighties, in the days when sextants were still used more than unreliable SatNavs, in the days when many cruisers were still distrustful of gadgetry and cruising boats were fairly simple and functional, he bought his first boat for our first family voyage that took us from England to New York via the European Coast, the Canary Islands and the

Caribbean. My father began to drill us about the many aspects of the sailing life from the time we first set foot on deck, and one of his main issues was water. All the way down the European coast, where all you had to do was turn left and head for any harbor for more water if you ran out, we still had to practice going without to be prepared for the potentially desperate times that lay ahead.

Among all the uses for salt water we discovered and explored, figuring out how to calculate a potable ratio of salt water to fresh water for boiling pasta was invaluable on a boat where both the failed freshwater pump and the kitchen hand pump that wouldn't prime easily went purposely unrepaired to facilitate frugality. We could drink as much tea and eat as many noodle soups we wanted, but suggesting a weekly freshwater rinse for the hair would have been received as a request nearly as ludicrous as asking for ice cream on a boat with no refrigeration. What, are you kidding? You want to waste fresh water to rinse your hair when we are surrounded by ocean? Keep dreaming, kiddo. And dream my sisters and I did, with our long hair, until we arrived in harbors with public showers.

Then came the Atlantic crossing, the big one where we could be at sea for weeks, even months if we got dismasted, said my father almost eagerly. He filled the fuel and water tanks while my sister and I made sure we had enough books to last forever because with my dad, we couldn't rule out that possibility. The trip from Gran Canaria to Guadeloupe ended up taking a modest twenty-four days because of some long-lived calms and strict conservation rules that applied to fuel and engine use as well. I can't remember how many gallons that boat carried, but she was a 38-footer designed for long-distance cruising, so the tanks must have been fairly substantial, yet we even had to brush our teeth in salt water for the crossing. When we got to Guadeloupe, those tanks had been barely touched; there was still enough for a Pacific crossing, because we children knew how to abide by my father's strict adherence to self-discipline.

Of course, there was no end to the ribbing he got for his

extreme ways, but two years later, when I left on a circumnavigation on my own boat, I took some of these ways with me. With only forty gallons of water in tanks and ten gallons in jerry cans, I made crossings that lasted up to fifty days, and, thanks to the ocean, managed to always stay clean. My cat and I never went thirsty, either, but several times, my Swiss stockpiling genes kicked in and I became concerned enough to rig a bucket underneath the main boom during heavy rains to increase the already healthy safety margin and my peace of mind.

Years later, on a week-long charter in Thailand's Phangnga Bay, I skippered a boat for a group of women. There was nowhere to fill the tanks during the trip, there were no jerry cans aboard for lugging any water, and I hadn't worked enough yet in the capacity of captain to be able to command anything near the authority my father had wielded over us. I wanted all the ladies to be happy, and when my feeble requests for bathing and doing dishes with salt water went largely unheeded, I just gritted my teeth and cringed every time I heard the water pump go on until, on the last day, there was nothing left to pump.

The ladies weren't being disobedient; it was more than that. It was a combination of me not feeling self-confident enough about my knowledge to assert it strongly, and these ladies' inability to radically ratchet back on the consumption of something we take for granted, which must be unlearned. The Swiss Army and my father's years of independent traveling in desert regions had taught him how to ration, how it's always better to learn how to live with the minimum than to run out. Without becoming quite as radical—I've never asked anyone to brush their teeth with salt water—I knew how bathing and doing dishes might be nicer with fresh water, but the salty stuff works very well, too. I can't say I would have known this, though, without having spent so many years at sea, cruising.

I never wanted to run out of water again, least of all with nine women on a boat, and in the Grenadines, a new and more mature version of me stood at the helm. Cruising isn't just about navigation, sail handling, and engine maintenance, I told them. It's a way of life that uses available resources and an economy of living we rarely get exposed to on land, especially in the United States. I showed them how wonderfully some soaps will lather up in sea water, how great it is to be able to sit on the aft swim platform and soap up, then to jump overboard and stay in the warm tropical water for as long as necessary to really get clean, without standing in a tiny head, using a trickle and feeling guilty because the electrical pump is a loud tattletale and the captain has good hearing. Then, with the deck shower, I allowed them to rinse off the salt water at the end—without the encumbrance of soap, this never uses much more than a pint. Best of all, I told them, with a bath off the stern, one never has to wipe down a stinky head, one of the most unpleasant things to do immediately after getting clean.

They also learned how resilient dishes, cutlery and pots and pans can be, how these items don't even need a freshwater rinsing if they're dried properly. The initial response was pretty doubtful, but by the end of our ten days, the biggest skeptics were washing and drying dishes with bucketfuls of water without a second thought. On our last day, except for the one woman who had never put her toes in the water, we were all jumping in, lathering up, jumping back in to get rid of the soap, and lightly rinsing off with a stern shower as if it were the most normal thing to do, which it is when you are surrounded by beautifully clear and warm ocean water. We returned to the dock having emptied only three of the four water tanks, well within the safety margin, not only with clean dishes, clean decks, and nine clean women, but seventy-five dollars ahead of the game.

Trash

As I write letters with final travel details for the next crew who will join me for a late-May sail among the Greek Islands, Earth Day has passed, and spring is coming to where I live. The snow has melted and before the tall grasses and undergrowth of summer hide everything, the garbage boneheads have been chucking out their car windows all winter is glaringly obvious. Wrappers, bottles, cans, packaging, plastic, glass, foam, and metal are everywhere.

On some stretches of road, there is enough flotsam and jetsam to fill seven garbage bags and to earn over ten dollars from returnables. I know, because this year, the sight really bugged me and I just had to get out there to clean it. I slipped down embankments, sloshed through swamps, and swore, thinking about the trashing of the planet, and my own guilt for contributing to it made me push harder, to pick up even more.

Very early on, not taking responsibility for my own garbage was associated with a scolding, or a Hollywood Indian surveying a pile of rubbish with a tear rolling down his cheek. But that was on land. At sea, from the people who were my teachers in my formative sailing years, I learned to litter. This was justified because cans became homes for fish, and if we poked holes into our garbage bags, they were supposed to sink, and biodegradables like paper and organic matter, well, they were biodegradable. The ocean wasn't really Earth, and if we even bothered to stop and think about it, we figured it was big enough to absorb the waste. We'd go on to look for perfectly pristine anchorages and grumble indignantly when they were difficult to find—only other people's garbage ever drifted ashore.

One day, a friend set me straight. Littering is never okay. Never, even on the ocean. He spent most of his life on boats and until the ocean claimed him, he was fanatical about leaving a clean wake, and I've never forgotten his passionate concern for the future of the environment as we know it. Now, I pay for my past sins every spring with pairs of gloves and garbage bags.

This always happens around the same time I go to Greece, so all my recent trash gathering and ranting has reminded me of the five women from a large mid-western city who once joined me for a trip on a boat named OUZO. They showed up on the dock near Athens with "ouzo" T-shirts, each "o" in the word colored as a hungover, bleary, red eyeball. This was the only group I ever had who was perfectly content to spend the first night in the huge marina, surrounded by the sounds of roaring cars, boat motors, a blaring disco in the distance, and steps away from a late night dockside bar. It was perfect for them, and I didn't mind either.

For me, a night in Athens is time for visiting with friends I only get to see once a year. When they brought me back a couple of hours before it was time to wake up and cast off for the islands, the last thing I expected to see was all my ladies at the dockside bar. As far as they were concerned, it wasn't even close to bedtime. When I turned to go grab a few winks, my friends said, "Hey, you can't leave them here like this. They're your responsibility."

I looked at the group, dancing with equally inebriated Adonis-types, saw their cameras lying around on the bar, their purses draped over chair backs. I turned to these professional skipper friends who knew all about taking care of visitors to the country that honored Dionysus. "What do I do?" I asked. "Carry them across the plank?"

"Yes. You must carry them across."

I looked at the five grown women. "But how? They're not gonna want to be carried."

We huddled and discussed my dilemma while one woman did a Queen Nefertiti dance around us. I decided I wasn't carrying anyone, but I would round up whoever wanted to return to the boat. Four pairs of ouzo-reddened eyes followed me back. As the first glimmers of dawn began to compete with the city lights, there was a misstep and a shuffle on the gangplank.

"Oops," giggled Queen Nefertiti, who reached back and let a purse slide from her fingers just as I offered to carry it across. I don't remember hearing a splash as the bag disappeared in slow motion, beneath the white stern, into shadows concealing the worst corner of one of the filthiest harbors I know.

The other two women fell against the railing and looked down into the darkness. "I think a camera wuth in that bag," one slurred, as she headed for her cabin.

Great. As far as I could see, I had only two choices. Either I dropped my own body into this scummy pit at first light so we could leave sooner, or we could try and locate a diver who worked on Sundays. But wait. What about the boat hook? I ran aboard, grabbed it, and began fishing around for the bag, blindly. The hook bumped cans and bottles, snagged bits of plastic bags and paper, and jostled sea urchins riding some of the partially submerged rubbish, knocking bits and bobs up against the boat hull. Disgusting. A swim seemed inevitable and I had just started preparing myself psychologically for the most odious of duties when the hook came up with a strap, quite literally saving my skin.

This used to be a good story to tell about ouzo and the incredibly good fortune that got between me and a toxic swim, but in the throes of my latest anti-littering fervor, one image in particular from that night stands out: the sight of a horrifying amount of waste accumulated in just one marina. Our trash is a universal problem (there is plenty even orbiting in the atmosphere above us), it's overwhelming and terrible. And, at sea, even if we make the decision to reduce consumption and re-cycle, and save everything else for disposal on land, chances are good it'll all end up on a garbage barge headed back out to sea anyway. To varying degrees, leaving a trail of refuse is part of the human condition, and one week after I cleaned my stretch of road, is has been re-peppered with fresh debris.

But, now that I'm on a spring cleaning jag, I'm wondering if there is a way to get a rake through airline security next month, or if they come in telescopic models, because I know this place in Greece that needs cleaning. I also know where to get some good ouzo when we're done so we can dance instead of worry-ing about how long it will take for it to be replaced by a new mess.

Relief

Literally, it happened somewhere toward the end of the eleventh hour. Minutes shy of the twelfth, I received the bi-monthly email from Bob Bitchin: "I hate to say it," he wrote, "but it's time. Why don't you write about the relief that comes with the end of a voyage?"

There I was, panicking, because once again so much had been put off until the last minute. I was scrambling to pack and make all the preparations necessary to leave my house, kids, and pets for two weeks in the middle of winter, and some masochistic streak in me demanded I check my e-mail, as if there were an extra minute to answer questions, much less to write entire articles! How un-Thai-mely!

The next morning, I was off to lead a ten-day sea and land tour of Thailand's Phuket and Phangnga Bay on its eastern flank. Under normal circumstances, say, if I were the customer and not the leader, I would have been too excited to eat or sleep on the eve of a trip to the other side of the world. It used to be that way as a kid, when all I had to worry about was how to pack. But, I've grown up and taken on responsibility for others and under that pressure, I was shuffling around the house, muttering, "This, too, shall pass. In two short weeks I'll be home again."

Anxiety and relief are quite intimately related and it would be incestuous for the two to share the same bed. They occupy separate rooms in the same house, close yet never together, and because one always precedes the other, I was in the middle of a visit with Anxiety when Bob's message arrived. For those who feel anxious about leaving home, there are many reasons: fear of spending too much money, fear of air travel, trains and cars, fear of malicious, foreign microbes, fear of not being anywhere that feels as safe as home. It all boils down to fear of every size and shape. Mine happens to be a fear of boats, which isn't such a good thing when boat-related work is a large part of how I bring to the table the kind of food my boys are willing to eat.

I've learned well enough to know what I'm doing; a lot of water has passed under keels driven by me. Put me in any boat show seminar and I'm able to understand most of what I hear. I can read *Moby Dick* or *Longitude* and comprehend the relevance of all the nautical and navigational references. I've learned a technical thing or two, but above all, the sea has taught me how to respect that which is beyond my control, the sort of respect that doesn't differ much from fear, and fear begets anxiety. Boats are built to sail oceans, not to stay in ports, and to deliberately take on the challenge of an environment where the most thorough preparation can sometimes be reduced to the same thing as minimal preparation always scares me.

On the day Bob furnished me with a subject to ponder, five ladies, a boat chartered for a week, hotel reservations, and rental cars were waiting, and I had no choice but to keep plodding along, crossing off items on the to-do list. Trusting everything would work out as usual, and remembering that fourteen days and two weeks don't add up to large numbers on the big canvas, I boarded the first plane on the 23-hour-long series of flights leading to Phuket.

The separation pangs I felt upon leaving my house was comparable to the emotional gauntlet I've run so often before, every time an anchor has been hauled in and a bow has been pointed seaward for another passage after saying goodbye to dependable harbors, friends, stores, and havens that have become safe and familiar. The subtle irony here is that anything can always happen anywhere, and nothing is permanently dependable, whether I'm intentionally heading into the great watery unknown, or if I think I'm safe at home. Safety is an illusion and perhaps it's better to challenge it sometimes, to see how far we can go, to learn about the stuff we are made of. And, maybe if I keep repeating this to myself, then one day I'll fully believe it, too, and leaving will stop being so difficult.

Once the first step into a voyage has been taken, though, the anxiety of anticipation takes a back seat to the experience itself, to the day-to-day reality of living it. In Phuket, I met the ladies and the captain of a boat we had fully expected to bareboat, a wild Aussie woman who was reluctant to let us take her boat cobbled together by all sorts of jury-rigged arrangements without her. This ended up being a good decision on her part when the steering went on day three and she had to spend a morning in the hole under the cockpit, realigning lines, chains, and sprockets of an arrangement only an owner could understand.

Before that, we participated in the first day of a three-day-long regatta until someone opened a hatch and in-flu-Enza. Half the boat checked out with Ralph and the twenty-four-hour flu. Boy, were they sick, and boy was I glad I wasn't.

For one week, we sailed Phangnga Bay, weaving a path through the magical splendor of nubby, jungle-covered, and cliffy islets connected to the mainland by hordes of longtails, the specialized indigenous canoe-like vessel of the Thai fisherman with huge, stern-mounted engines and long shafts extending out over the surface in order to navigate the shallow waters. A pack of them cruising through an anchorage sounds like a pack of Harleys, as the engines are unhampered by annoying mufflers. We visited and snorkeled in Krabi, Phi Phi (pronounced pee pee) Islands, and Koh Rok Nok. The last three days ashore were spent on Patong Beach, shopping and filling up on the delicious Thai food before the long trip home.

Indeed, in two weeks time, Thailand became part of my past

and a great success, despite the few glitches that were resolved before becoming the essential ingredients of a better story for Bob. The beauty of any trip is that rarely will everything go wrong all at once and, in hindsight, the whole package always has a beginning, a middle, and an end. For me, beginnings are always reserved for anxiety, middles are for experience, problems and troubleshooting, and only once the beginning and middle have been combined to form a past can room be made for the ending, and relief. Yes, this metaphor of the voyage is one I also consistently carry into the challenges of existence between actual trips. No matter how beginnings and middles come together and play out, I am always looking to revisit endings and ultimately, the sweet relief they bring.

Goodbyes

It isn't my intention to be all sad and melancholic by bringing up the subject, but it has been a season of goodbyes. Nicholas just said goodbye to his classmates who are being split up as they head into third grade, and he is sorrowful, feeling the separation pangs. Sam, the five year old, just said goodbye to his day care of the last three years before heading into a new school and kindergarten, and he has been asking if he can go back for just one more day. I am graduating from my own school of the past three years and I already miss the deadlines, the dialogue, and the intimacy I felt with my classmates.

I reassure the kids, telling them we will revisit the day care, the kids in other classes, just as I tell myself that I will keep in touch with the friends I've made. Maybe they believe me, maybe they don't. I know if I believe what I'm saying, I'm kidding myself. No matter how good the intentions, how close the bonds may be, once the spell of an environment that unites a group of people together is broken and the group disbands, the friendships alter and change with time, fading and fuzzing around the edges as new friends and activities rush in to fill the empty space. Goodbyes don't have to be depressing, I tell the kids, they are just part of life, part of growing up and moving on.

In May, a month before the end of all our school years, I helped to lead a flotilla in the Greek Islands, and the boat I skippered had seven other women aboard. For ten days, we got seasick, reefed the sails, pounded into 35-knot winds, dragged anchor, docked, provisioned, made repairs, ate, bathed, and talked confidentially. From every corner of the United States and England, too, we brought our stories to this comparatively small space of 58 feet (on deck) and shared them. When time came to hand the keys back over to the charter agent, we all knew a lot about each other's habits, moods, and personalities. As we said goodbye, I felt the familiar tugging in my heart and belly, the one that precedes the withdrawal from people I have grown to care about, and this bittersweet sense of emptiness and loss still catches me by surprise.

I have acquainted myself with many different farewells. Hello, goodbye, and thank-you are the first words I learn in every language, and sometimes, they remain the only words. In Turkish, farewell is pronounced more or less like this: *alla smalla dik*—easy enough to remember. For all the different ways to say it, somebody once said that to say any kind of goodbye is to die a little. I believe it. The certainty that with every goodbye a new hello will follow is of small comfort when we are actually closing the book on yet another chapter of friendship. But, it is worthwhile to remember goodbyes lead to new hellos, which will then also turn into goodbyes spiraling toward another round of hellos.

The sailor who wanders about the planet from port to port becomes very familiar with partings, even more so than the average person ashore. It is a fact of sailing life, of any traveling or nomadic life. As I write this, in harbors around the world, inter-cockpit friendships are being formed, nurtured, and cemented; at the same time, oceans around the world are full of boats who have just left people behind, people who may never see each other again in spite of all good intentions and promises. How many people are out there with whom I felt so bonded, as if neither time nor distance could ever erode our amity? And, with how many of them am I still in touch? Not many at all. There are a few good correspondents who have kept up with return mail, if even on a yearly basis, but mainly, we have drifted apart. This isn't to say we wouldn't greet each other like long lost relatives if we were to cross paths again, picking up where we left off, but this would be a rare and wonderful thing, because people grow and change, and we can never step in the same river twice.

Perhaps worldwide access to Internet cafes, and the more affordable communications systems that can now be rigged on boats—so that it was possible for my husband to fax and call us from the high seas with his position and news on a recent delivery—will make it easier to keep in touch. However, letters, telephone calls, and e-mails can only do so much, and they can't replace the reality of actually being together.

Many years ago, I read *Out of Africa* by Isak Dinesen. I don't remember the story very well, but one line left a lasting impression. After a lifetime spent on a plantation with neighbors, farmhands, and a support system she loved and relied upon, Dinesen had to return to Europe. As she was leaving, she wondered if now that she had a song of Africa, would Africa also have a song of her? Of course it would.

If the snippets of memories I have of people from all around the world, and even from my school close to home, partake in any kind of universal similarity, then there are as many others out there who have snippets of memories that include me. And, as we sail on, move on, we continue to build the collage of snippets with new friends and experience. All together, then, we each have our own song of individualized memories.

Nicholas and Sam are saying their first goodbyes and learning about the sadness and eventual acceptance. Though it doesn't get easier, at least I know what to tell them to expect. I've learned to go with farewells, even to savor them as the price we pay for having connected with people. The more often it happens, the more the memories gather. These become the food for later thought and reflection, the perfect occupation for the sailor at sea who has just bid farewell to one harbor with the course set for another.

PART 3

Contretemps

Lessons

Many years ago, I was twenty years old, alone on my boat with fifteen thousand miles laid under the keel toward completing a single-handed circumnavigation. There was still plenty of water left to cross, nearly half the planet, with a reserve of learning opportunities as bottomless as the sea itself. Off the coast of Sri Lanka, en route for Djibouti, once again, a lesson reminded me of what can happen when manuals aren't consulted and instructions aren't properly followed.

The stuffing box, a plug of sorts that guides the propeller shaft through the hull, popped out of the stern tube and the Indian Ocean became the unwelcome teacher, gushing its way in the bilge through the pipe-like hole. With the help of a screwdriver and a pocketknife, later lost to the flooded bilge, I managed to cram the stuffing box back into the tube and tighten the hose clamp holding it there—temporarily. Intent on driving the lesson home, for more than two thousand miles of westward progress, every time I put the engine into gear, the stuffing box escaped, and the Indian Ocean forced its way back in.

The fault was all mine. I had literally invited the sea over and when she arrived, I called her an intruder. The stuffing box problem had nothing to do with the corrosive effects of time, or the routine breakdown of sacrificial parts that weren't meant to last. It was completely due to a lack of attention, a sort of carelessness essential to my unintentional, yet, stubbornly applied method of learning by making a mistake first, then cleaning up the mess. Easily overwhelmed by mechanics, I could only admire from afar the merit of a more proactive approach, and the stuffing box never made the grade on my maintenance list.

Once it seized itself onto the shaft, however, I consulted the engine manual, which clearly stated it should have been greased regularly via a small nipple. In hindsight, I could remember staring down at the protrusion with absolutely no idea as to how the grease would get transferred and what tool would ever affix itself onto that piece, if it could even be found. The obstacles between me and proper maintenance created a minefield of potential pitfalls—grease guns incompatible with nipples, greases of uncertain viscosity, trips to too many foreign hardware stores with clerks shaking their heads uncomprehendingly—enough to make me completely ignore the stuffing box until the day it copped an attitude.

The subsequent weeks of attempted repairs in ill-equipped countries, the amount of inconvenience and worry it gave me, outweighed the relatively small investment of time it would have taken to prevent the whole aggravation. It also forced me to pay attention, to really investigate and become familiar with the operation of a stuffing box and its relationship to the shaft and propeller in a way I would have never understood as fully as I did when it stopped working.

Some people are really good at absorbing and understanding theories and applying them to real life models. Others need to experience the real life model before beginning to understand the abstraction of the theory, and this path requires a lot of room for error. It was the route I took then, it is the route I still take now, despite all the chances I've been given to change direction. I ought to be the poster girl for learning from mistakes.

Take the subject of celestial navigation, for another example. During the year before I set sail, I took a course in a classroom full of guys who nodded thoughtfully and intelligently after only one demonstration of a tilting plum orbiting around an orange while my brain got hotter and hotter. I didn't get it at all. Declination? Azimuth? Greenwich hour angle? I flunked the course so big time, I can't even remember taking the final exam.

I shrugged my shoulders and photocopied my father's dummy manual with the calculation process broken down into an easy-to-follow formula without all the theory. I was only eighteen and hadn't yet scared myself witless often enough to not trust I would be able to figure it out. Being in the middle of the ocean and not knowing my position will be the best motivation to learn, I told myself. Sure enough, after several passages spent working with the formula daily and getting lost and found, I finally did come to understand what the instructor had been talking about in that classroom of humming fluorescent lighting.

I have often thought about those guys who took the class with me, wondering if their frames of reference only consisted of dividers, rulers, and being able to conceptualize trigonometric lines and angles. Or, had they been able to visualize the sun chasing and leading a boat west as it cast shadows on the water through patches of clouds? Could they have been seeing the moon rising over the horizon to brighten a windy, dark night? Were they able to feel the oppressive heat when the sun's declination matched the latitude? On a westerly course, did bedtime get later every night until it got recalibrated by the next time zone? I couldn't have learned to navigate any other way, without actually living, sleeping, and eating by the progress of the heavenly navigational aids, and I now know this would hold true for many others as well. It's just another method of learning, visual and empirical rather than theoretically cognitive.

I see this when I teach sailing. To many novices, the points of sail and how course and sail trim are interdependent are as incomprehensible as Local Hour Angle once was for me. No matter how many times I draw the circle, describing head winds, beam winds, and jibing through tail winds, to beam winds on the opposite side, and tacking back through head winds, the

quizzical and frustrated looks persist. Physically tacking and jibing boats full of nomenclature—sheets, booms, blocks, winches,
bows, sterns—through the points of sail can make it even more
confusing. I usually end the lessons by saying, "Look, forget
the words and theory. What you need to do now is to rent a little daysailer and muck about in your area. You need to feel the
wind, play with the sails and the tiller, and see how the three in-
teract." For many of us, no amount of sophistry will make a jibe
or a backwinded jib more understandable than repetition of the
actual experience and mistakes.

The way I learned about stuffing boxes, navigation, and
points of sail used to make me feel guilty and defensive, as if
preparation and study had been an option for me, as if it were a
matter of the right and wrong way. I've come to realize it isn't. If
I'd insisted on preparing by the book first, and if I'd worried
about everything the books said, I'd still be in the armchair trying to understand the words. Real life messes have taught me
how to be a decent sailor, navigator, mechanic, and ultimately, a
good troubleshooter. Each one has taught me what different
problems look like and how they may be prevented or fixed, in
order to clear the decks for unannounced visits from new trou-
blesome guests because, you know, they've got my number and
they keep coming.

Precision

It all started two fields away from my house, over a cup of coffee. My impulsive neighbor, Fritz, had just purchased a used small sailboat, and he asked if the professional sailor and licensed captain next door could help with the maiden voyage.

"I'll come and get you in half an hour," Fritz called, as I walked away from his house to get ready. I've never gone out for a sail twenty minutes away from my home, and it took a little while to realize that I needed nothing for the afternoon beyond the clothes on my back. No passport, no food, no tools, not even a wallet. How easy was that? When Fritz's rusty old pick up rolled up the driveway with the sailboat and trailer in tow, I hopped onto the seat next to his daughter, Margo, and her friend, Francesca, and we set off for Lake Fairlee.

I've sailed tens of thousands of miles on all different sizes of boats on all kinds of seas and oceans, and I was so jittery about this little afternoon jaunt I made Fritz stop at the Fairlee Diner for lunch just to buy some more time to think things through. It was pretty ridiculous. If I have a reputation for anything worth mentioning, it is for being a sailor, even though the fact I know how to do anything on a boat still astonishes me. As a sailor, I also know how boats, small or large, have a unique way of introducing unannounced lessons, and how it is always a good idea to be prepared for this eventuality. Oblivious to my concern, Fritz and the girls chattered and the pick up truck clattered, while I listened to the sound of a halyard banging against the horizontal mast bumping along behind us, mentally walking through my first launching of a small boat.

When we pulled into the parking area next to the ramp, a group of scuba divers had just come back in with a load of Eurasian milfoil, a weed that has been slowly invading the lakes around here. Randy, the dive leader and a neighbor who has read many sailing books, including mine, chuckled as Margo and Francesca high tailed it out of our immediate area, certain Fritz and I were about to embarrass them. Amid a flurry of maiden voyage laughs, the fun began.

In the parking lot, Fritz followed my lead as we fit together the pieces of the familiar puzzle. It all came together flawlessly, and as always, I began to feel the satisfied surprise that comes with rediscovering I can do something. Designs may change or differ, one from the other, but the fundamentals of all sailboats are the same, and it was neat to be able to do everything manually, for once. The two of us raised the mast and attached it to chainplates with mini-turnbuckles. With one hand pulling, and the other hand feeding, the main was hoisted up the mainmast groove, and the jib flew up the forestay. Skinny sheets were attached to the foot of the jib, and a downhaul doubled as the mainsheet that led back to the tiller.

Fritz's Precision 14 was now riding the trailer, fully assembled with sails fluttering in a soft breeze as the next step was discussed. Neither of us had ever backed up a pickup with a trailer—down a narrow ramp, no less; happily, Fritz was the designated driver. When he got behind the wheel, I signaled and after many turns, the wheels lined up for a straight shot to the water.

"Okay! Come on down," I called, and watched as the boat passed me and eased toward the lake. All was good in the hood—for a couple of seconds. Then, it wasn't. Nowhere near the water, the stern of the boat started to lift up, off the trailer, airborne. What the heck? I looked around for an explanation, then up. Oh, man. Who'd've thunk? Directly above the trailer and the loading ramp, a crew of planning geniuses from the electrical company had run the power lines. The mast was hung up on the lowest and fortunately, the most insulated wire, levering the stern up higher with every inch Fritz rolled back.

"Stop!" I shrieked. "Pull forward . . . now!" Fritz obeyed, and the boat settled back down onto the trailer bed with a mast that was now raked distinctly forward, a racing rig in reverse.

Okay, it wasn't the end of the world. Randy and his cronies were gone and we were the sole witnesses to this folly. We played it cool and the mast and sails came down, to be raised again on the other side of the power lines, while bobbing on the water. The job was executed perfectly even though I had some misgivings. What else were we overlooking? Randy came back, saw the reconfigured mast, chortled some more, and suddenly thought to loan us some life jackets. When it was time to set sail, Margo and Francesca reluctantly rejoined us.

I stood in the water clutching the stern and instructed Fritz on how to hold the tiller and jib sheet to steer us out of the shallows. It took several tries before the rudder could be flipped all the way down, and we were headed for the center of the lake just as the first drops of rain began to fall on our shakedown cruise. Well, I joked, this wasn't the ocean. If anything went dreadfully wrong, the August water was warm and the distance to shore would be always close enough for a swim.

But as we tacked up-lake and back down-lake, two strange things happened that made the idea of swimming much less funny. First, a steady flow of water came up through the centerboard slot, which seemed like a major design flaw, especially since the cockpit wasn't draining. Second, the boat wouldn't respond properly to the wind. On the starboard tack, under full sail, the boat heeled over to starboard. This defied logic and all of my attempts to demonstrate the sport of sailing to Margo and Francesca. Wind is supposed to push a boat away and down, not pull it up. The completely uninspired girls, Fritz, and I clambered from one side of the flooded cockpit to the other, countering a heel that had nothing to do with the wind and a point of sail. Mystified, we sailed the lemon back and forth, with less and less freeboard and more and more unexplainable heeling, through a fleet of dinghy sailors, and finally back to the landing.

Relieved, the girls jumped ashore while Fritz and I bagged the sails and thought about pulling the boat up the ramp with the mast raised in order to straighten it back out against the power line. It seemed like a good idea for a minute until we noticed that while a steady flow was pouring out the stern drain, the water level in the cockpit hardly budged. After emptying several bathtubs worth of lake, I realized the hole in the stern wasn't the outlet end of a cockpit drain, but an inlet feeding directly into the space between the deck and cockpit mold and the hull.

The plugs that came with the boat were in the wrong holes, and if the boat hadn't been unsinkable, we really would have been swimming. Hmmm. The only thing left to do with that day was to chalk it up as another lesson, go home, and be thankful Fritz was still a boat owner. One month later, after consulting with the boat's former owner and other local experts, the questions are still unanswered. So, if anybody knows how those plugs and cockpit drains work . . . you can find me out back, straightening a mast.

Fouled Prop

⌒

Several years ago, my neighbor, Kathy, her boy, another friend, Maggie, my two boys, and I, chartered a 36-foot boat and circumnavigated Tortola. As usual, I was captain (incidentally, at this point in my life, I fantasize about being crew), my two friends were complete novice sailors, and the ages of the boys—four and two—speak for themselves as far as their contribution to the vacation was concerned. The little bodies, diapers, and stuffed animals falling overboard only added to the list of concerns and my eyes and ears had to be in many places at once. It was the second day out and the eyes blinked when they shouldn't have.

After a routine day of beating and tacking into the blasting January trades that funnel between the British Virgin Islands, we were closing in on the next anchorage. We rolled up the furling main and jib and suddenly, the engine stopped dead with no warning hiccups or alarms. The sound of a stalling engine has haunted many a night, turning perfectly good dreams into nightmares, but this time I was wide awake. It didn't take long to spot a previously undetected line leading from a forward cleat to what could be only one place under the boat. The propeller. I had done the unthinkable. In all my years of sailing, I have made many mistakes, but this was the first time I had ever fouled a prop. It was very small comfort to know the situation could have been worse, much worse, on a lee shore for instance, because even if some times are better than others, there just is no good time for a fouling.

Yanking ineffectively on the taut dockline, we drifted downwind, a boat full of women and whining children, as I ran through my options. I didn't want to attempt tacking through a somewhat crowded anchorage up to a mooring with a furling main and inexperienced crew, and the dinghy and outboard didn't have the power to muscle us upwind, through the waves. There was only one thing to do and that was to unfoul the prop, immediately, and doing so was up to me.

I put on the mask and snorkel and eased myself into the water at the stern where the swim platform bucked up and down in the waves. It's amazing how much more a boat seems to lurch about when viewed from sea level, especially when the necessity of going under several tons of bouncing fiberglass is imminent. Hanging off the stern, I would have gladly submitted to unanesthetized root canal if it meant I wouldn't have to dive under the aptly named SACAJAWEA.

Where were her two friends, Lewis and Clark, when they were needed? They would have dived for her. In the olden days, in tales of derring-do, men saved damsels in distress all the time. Hey, in the olden days, three women and three kids alone on a sailboat with a fouled prop would have been the result of a fatal tragedy involving all the men, the stuff history is made of, and more fantasy on my part. The mask was leaking. Emptying it and trying to put it back on without catching any hair, I looked around one last time for an approaching knight astride a dinghy; there was nothing but heaving swells, five people and a charter company depending on me, and the receding promise of a comforting anchorage as we continued to drift, all because of a foolish oversight.

I had no choice but to sink beneath the waves that lifted, dropped, and thudded against the hull, and to follow the line, hand over hand, to the prop. Holding the mouthful of air I gulped before diving, I pulled hard on the line, to no avail. Never before had I so appreciated the appropriateness of the word "foul" to describe a clump of line wound around a shaft and permanently wedged into itself. In the end, it was countless dives and breathless hacking with a serrated steak knife from the galley that chopped the mess away, charter boats being woefully ill-equipped in the tool department. As the last bit of fiber floated off, I clambered back aboard, shivering and promising myself this would never happen again.

Minutes later, the day, no, the whole vacation was saved, as the engine rumbled back to life and brought us to the safety of another anchorage where, over cups of tea and hot chocolate, Maggie, Kathy, the kids, and I practiced the first incarnation of a story with a happy ending. I'd be a liar if I said I wasn't proud of myself, which leads to the second moral of this tale. For the last five days of the charter, I invented and rehearsed stories to tell the charter company representative, just in case the propeller had been damaged, only to chicken out and fess up to her in the end. It turned out fouled props are all too routine in the industry. So are the subsequent beachings and shipwrecks of my other nightmares, problems I never want to face or handle. Now, having just relived this experience again, tonight I am content to count my blessings.

Pride

❦

The boat's name was BLOOM; we changed it to BOOM. "We had a smashing time," one autograph says. Another says, "rock n' roll." Another says, "shit happens." Indeed, it does, and the chunk of inscribed fiberglass sitting on my kitchen table serves as a reminder. No, I've said to curious guests. No, it's not a piece of a cast. It's part of the boat I skippered in Greece, signed by the great crew who lived the experience with me.

The biggest boat I ever skippered and my first rock met on the same trip, on the first day of the trip, on the first day of a trip with nine women who wanted to learn how to sail from me, the first day of a ten-day trip with nine lives in my allegedly competent hands. Nine lives, my biggest boat and a rock all came together in Greece, the country where I have sailed the most, where I know and like the waters, the islands, and the weather almost as well as I know and like the charter company to whom I had to make the humiliating report. The day after it happened, I was sitting on a wall in Siros, waiting for the phone, head in hands. Eyeing an enormous cross perched on a distant peak, I told my friend Jill, I would climb up there and carry it down to the harbor if the clock would then turn back two days. My pride was terribly wounded, worse than the boat.

Facing the music and calling the guys at the charter base with a description of the modified keel was one of the hardest things I have ever done and they didn't make the confession any easier by not believing I wasn't joking. And, no matter how my feverish mind tried to cut and paste the possible excuses into something else, I was still responsible for the one thing a boat was never meant to do: hit a stationary and hard object. Period. The damage was done and I had to come to terms with it.

The rock was inevitable. Having been engaged in this sailing occupation with inherent risks for a living, I always suspected chances were good that one day my nearly perfect record would get a red mark. Now that the worst had happened, I battled ugly emotions—guilt and self-criticism. The rock was clearly charted, and I was gabbing away when the keel boomed and bounced, glasses shattered, rigging shuddered, my heart nose-dived. I looked overboard and saw the rock that had appeared under our port side, an unforgettable mass of liquid browns and reds under the swirling water, right where it was supposed to be. At the end of that day, I wrote in my journal, "I can't help but relive the shock over and over again, the pounding as we hit. I'll remember it forever, how I sat there in the seconds leading up to it, off a course I should have been paying closer attention to with others at the wheel, oblivious to what was about to happen."

I see now, with the clarity of hindsight and knowing the boat was quickly repaired and continues to earn her keep, and because we had a great trip anyway, that self-recriminations and guilt are the first step to recovery, to get to a place where you don't feel like people are pointing you out anymore as "the one who hit the rock." And, there is no place like Greece to recover from such a blow. Another thing is for sure: there's nothing like having an accident to bring out everyone else's tales of horror. The good-natured ribbing and stories I heard in the following week from my Greek skipper friends scattered around the islands finally managed to put the whole experience into a better perspective. It wouldn't be all about me forever.

All manner of real-life nautical nightmares were relived, paling mine in comparison, from flaming instrument panels, to entire sets of teeth being knocked out, to gaping head wounds, to boats being completely lost. The best advice came from an older, seasoned guy who said that as we age, our pride takes so many knocks the inflated importance vested in it eventually deflates. It comes with the territory of being experienced. "Pride," he said, when I complained that mine had suffered more damage than the boat, "is over-rated. Build a bridge and get over it, Tania." His story wins the prize, too. On one of his trips, he engaged the autopilot for a quick visit to the head when a rock leaped out of nowhere and he found himself with the potty on top of the head attached to his neck.

A healthy respect and awareness of the inevitability of the unexpected, on the other hand, is very real for everyone, I found, not just me. My friends in Greece are hardcore sailors, taking groups out on charters all summer long, year in and year out, often in the howling meltemi winds. They sail fast, sleep little, party hard, and my impression of them is of a modern-day, Odysseus-like bunch of guys commanding the wine dark seas. During this trip, though, a couple of them let me see past this veneer of bravado as we talked about and shared our fears. My encounter with the rock may have prompted reflection on the sobering topic, but the ease with which the guys were able to relate belied how very close to the surface this fear lies.

"Obviously, I've been meeting every trip with more and more apprehension in the past couple of years, waiting for something to go wrong for good reason," I said to Jiorgos. "Yes," he exclaimed. "I feel the same. How long can the gods keep smiling on me?" How long?

I had already developed an uneasy relationship with this feeling during my own circumnavigation. Having already sailed 23,000 miles, the last 4,000 across the Mediterranean and Atlantic were my most daunting. Luck, wit, perseverance, vigilance, whatever it was that got me that far safely, could also abandon me suddenly. If disaster were in my cards, with every mile made closer to the final destination, I felt as if I were nearing the real moment of truth.

This promised moment of truth had leered so menacingly at another Athenian friend that he had traded in his foul-weather gear for a bartender's apron. Coincidentally, partly because of this fear, this trip was also meant to be our last official company trip. Jill and I had decided to fold in order to concentrate better on other aspects of our lives and, I thought, to quit while we were still ahead, as had my Greek friend.

We're still folding, but I figure the reset button has been pressed, the accident widening my horizons because I survived, hopefully wiser for it. My pride also recovered somewhat because of my crew, because of the nine women who trusted me from beginning to end, never questioning my decisions and competence as I grappled with shame. I discovered what it means to take a hit, stumble, and regain a more careful footing with another story to tell about a smashing time, with a splash of humility, on the rocks.

Squalls

Surfing downwind wave by wave, main boomed out to one side and jib poled out on the other, the miles tick by. A squadron of cottony clouds follow and overtake the boat, puffs of perfect whiteness to rival the sparkling crests of waves curling over and sprinkling spray over the cockpit as each one passes under the keel with a bubbly hiss. Flying fish leap from bumpy swells, soaring across the seas in flight from larger predators below. The dolphins enter, leaping and cavorting about, delighted with yet another beautiful day, keeping pace until, like fickle children, they tire and dart off to find another plaything. These are the ideal conditions of a trade wind run. There's nothing like a day such as this, the kind aspiring cruisers dream about and experienced sailors remember with the smug fondness that comes from knowing they have shared a communion with nature many others will never know.

But, wait. There's more. What's that smudge on the horizon, a smudge that is growing ever larger beneath a big anvil-shaped cloud? Oh yeah. Another side to nature is the first sign of a squall. That figures. How many times do sudden squalls come knocking out of the clear blue, when things couldn't be looking better? Fortunately, one redeeming feature of the squall is it won't spawn suddenly, appearing out of nowhere. Day or night, skies will get darker first, and heaviness in the air will announce an imminent change with a different smell, the distinctive metallic odor of wind mixed with rain.

Before a squall hits, there is time to close hatches, gather up laundry drying on lifelines, to prepare to shorten sails, or to drop them entirely, to gather up soap and other bathing equipment, and if the boat doesn't have a desalinator, time enough to rig up the water collection system, too. Thank God for some predictability because while we know squalls usually bring thunder, lightning, and wind, on the flip side, the pregnant clouds also hold enough moisture to both fill tanks and to take proper showers, hair and all.

As the leading edge approaches, the sky darkens ominously. The wind dies and comes back irregularly, in fits and spurts of gusts and calm; the boat loses speed and direction. When a line of distant angry whitecaps becomes visible, deployed from the grimmest looking corner of the sky, it is time to drop sail. Preventers are loosened, the boom and spinnaker pole are sheeted in, and Teflon slides rattle in the track as the sails pleat themselves downward in a rush of fabric. Lines are pulled inboard and swiftly coiled as the unbalanced boat stops making headway and begins to seesaw in the seas, a motion immediately followed by sounds emitting from below through the companionway. Cans roll drunkenly in their lockers, bottles clink together, doors unlatch and slam to and fro, thuds accompany missiles ejected from shelving, and the hope is none of this will mean damage to a favorite food or drink and a major cleanup. The atmosphere is charged with anticipation.

Sure enough, moments later, any trace of the sun that may have been visible ahead of the front disappears. The line of whitecaps catches up and the initial gust is a wallop. The first blast of wind is almost visible in force, grabbing the meager windage of the boat's hull and rigging and slamming it down in a headlock, broadside to the waves. Forty, fifty, or even sixty knots of wind, the actual figure is incidental. It's enough to know it is strong and dropping sail was the prudent thing to do.

Directly on the heels of the wind, a solid wall of rain bears down, preceded by seconds worth of heavy droplets, a paltry courtesy before the deluge hits mercilessly, flattening the seas. Where the wind hasn't succeeded to punch the boat into the water, the rain does. It thunders down and streams of heaven-borne water create gully washers along the deck, a stage-four rapid of hydraulics and eddies forming instantaneously as the unrestrained river gushes and collects sternward because only so much can leave through the scuppers at a time. The water level rises and begins to overflow, a Niagara Falls pouring over the toe rail. The water collection system works beautifully and the tanks are filling up faster than they would at any dock, as fast as the wide-mouth funnels permit.

The boat is kept heeled over and relatively steady by the wind. Wedged into a safe spot with hand and footholds on deck, out come the soap and shampoo. A shower feels great, such a welcome treat, and there's no need to conserve water. It's coming full bore and the only time limit is circumscribed by the capacity of the squall itself, which always depends. Since there's no way to forecast the duration of the shower, it's best to get soaping and shampooing out of the way in order to guarantee a thorough rinsing. There aren't many things worse than being all soaped up and having the freshwater supply cut off, when the disappointed body needs to be rinsed with buckets of the usual salty stuff, yet again.

On a trade wind crossing, squalls break up the monotony of perfection. Just as life settles into a comfortable routine, they come along to stir things up, to raise the level of excitement. They make the heart beat a little faster, the blood surge a little stronger, because something different is about to happen, and once the cloud looms directly behind the boat, there is no escaping the thrill. But, when it ends, when the rain eases, slowly dying to a fine drizzle, when the wind disappears and the boat begins to lurch in the agitated and erratic waves slapping up against the bottom of the hull, the excitement grows old fast.

The squall isn't so much fun anymore; it becomes a test of patience. The last puddles on deck swish out the scuppers; the mainsheet clatters as the boom swings showers of droplets from side to side, and the banging and clunking from below resumes to join the discordant symphony of annoying sounds. There is no point in resetting the sails until the trades fill back in from behind. Instead, it is better to do something, to keep busy by gathering up the water collecting system, closing the inlets, and waiting out the transitional moment, maybe even over a cup of tea.

Everything drips, but the boat is a salt free enclave of freshness and contrast in color—the droplets of water, the clean white decks, the dark wet wood, the sails and the mast all juxtaposed sharply against a backdrop of the sea and the lifting cloud cover. Then, the warming sun is back and the first gentle nudges of regular winds flutter the drenched ensign on the backstay. It's time to return to life as it was prior to the squall. The sails go up, the steering system is set, the miles resume ticking, and all is a little cleaner, if not better for the interlude, prepared for the next one.

Life Rafts

I probably shouldn't be admitting this so readily, but in the parking lot of the Portofino resort where the *Latitudes and Attitudes* Advanced Cruising Seminar was being held last month, I think I saw my first inflated life raft. I certainly have never seen it happen at sea, and since a sinking situation might be the last place you would want to see your first life raft inflation, it was a great lesson. It also made me think about my own history with life rafts.

When I first started sailing with my father twenty years ago, there was a life raft mounted on the deck of his Rival 38, and among all the other things we were being taught, he showed my brother, sister, and me how to deploy it. He was so persistent about two cardinal life raft rules that I can still recite his words today.

The first seemed obvious: "Always make sure the life raft is attached to the boat before throwing the canister overboard." In panic situations, the obvious will get forgotten, my father insisted when we laughed with the childlike certainty we'd *never* do anything so silly. The second rule wasn't as evident: "Always step *up* into a life raft," he drilled us, the implication being that your boat is almost under water if you have to step *up*, a sure sign that abandoning ship is the last resort.

A man of cautionary tales, my father had one to illustrate this rule. Once, a fleet participating in the English *Fastnet* race ran into and got overwhelmed by a storm of unpredicted strength. After the system had moved on, a bunch of boats were found bobbing on the leftover swells, minus all their crews and life rafts. The sailors had panicked, prematurely abandoning their boats, and tragically many were lost without a trace.

"Until there's nothing left but the life raft, the best place to be is on the big boat," he repeated many times, even as we crashed over, under, and through gargantuan waves a year later in a Gulf Stream storm that sank other boats in our vicinity.

Under the companionway steps, we had a go-bag, a cooler filled with extra water, candy bars, first aid supplies, fishing gear, and most importantly, a knife we were instructed to remember before abandoning ship. If we were certain the boat was going down, and if we had remembered to attach the life raft before deploying it, we needed to be sure to have a way to cut ourselves loose, my father said, backing up this lesson with yet another disaster story.

Standing on the blacktop outside of the seminar, looking at the six-man life raft that had been inflated for the class and imagining it bucking around on an ocean swell in howling winds, I remembered how eighteen years ago, I sailed 24,000 miles without a traditional life raft. Instead, the builders of my 26-foot boat had injected a rigid polyurethane foam into every inaccessible nook and cranny, and in each of the two lockers under the settee, I carried a yellow valise with a CO_2 inflatable balloon to help with emergency buoyancy. This was called theoretical positive flotation, and the idea was to make the boat itself into the life raft. If water suddenly began to find its way into the hull, the foam and balloons were intended to keep the boat afloat until I could trace the leak and make a repair with all my tools at hand.

It was a fabulous alternative system; it worked like a charm, theoretically, because I never actually had to test it out. Since the foam had been injected into spaces I was never meant to see, I didn't even know what it looked like. As time marched on, though, an alien and gooey brownish-yellow substance began to dribble down along the hull, pooling at the bottom of my lockers. Scraping up the sticky mess, I figured this was the rigid foam losing its rigidity, biodegrading, and turning into a housekeeping nuisance. As the persistent trickle challenged my idea of cleanliness, I idly wondered about the rate at which my positive flotation was disappearing, and if the balloons would be able to do the job alone, and if the CO_2 bottles would even work when and if the time ever came. But, really, I was more concerned about the additional cleaning chore than the threat to my survival in the event of a disaster.

Out in the middle of the ocean, the fact that I could sink seemed a much more remote possibility than getting hit on the head by the boom, something that happened to one friend, killing him instantly. In a storm, I was more concerned with falling overboard because of a misstep and a big wave than floundering. Whenever I felt out of sorts, I would remember how my mother had just died from a cancer, and that all kinds of things inside my body were conspiring to kill me. Because heart disease also runs in my family, any weird tingling on the left side of my body sent up the red flags. Throw in the threats of botulism, aneurysms, and poisonous rigid polyurethane vapors, and there was no room left to believe VARUNA, the hunk of solid fiberglass that was my home, would be my comeuppance.

That changed in the Mediterranean, a crossing during which I got hit by a ship, knocked down by a tremendous wave, and read Steve Callahan's survival story, *Adrift*. His description of the seventy-six days he spent in a life raft propelled me to get one of my own in Gibraltar, before an October North Atlantic crossing. With the canister tied down on the foredeck as a small measure of comfort, I weathered the kinds of storms that whipped up the thundering, hissing waves I was imagining in the Portofino parking lot.

I listened to the demonstrator tell the group that, thanks to modern technology and a new kind of EPIRB, we wouldn't have to spend very much time in this rubber raft. In coastal waters, we could count on being rescued within hours, and in the middle of the ocean, within days. Right. But, what if the EPIRB malfunctioned? What if a couple days turned into seventy-six days? Then what? As I looked at the logo that was displayed boldly on every feature of the life raft before us, from the tent to the bailing bucket and emergency rations bag, it hit me like the Nike swoosh.

In what could be my final days, those large block letters staring at me, a captive audience to all their lifesaving promises, would kill me before anything else. The seminar taught me about one more thing I will have on hand for the day when and if all the life raft theory becomes real. An indispensable item for any go-bag I will ever pack is a big, fat permanent magic marker to erase the logos, if it's the last thing I ever do.

Perfect Storm

The other day while my car was in the shop, I killed some time in the adjoining showroom and took a test drive with a salesman who was a former lobster boat captain. I asked about the scarcity of coastal lobsters these days, and he said his family's fleet went offshore to catch the critters, to Georges and Sable Banks, and beyond, to the Flemish Cap. The Flemish Cap! Wow. Until several years ago, unless you were a fisherman in the North Atlantic and knew all the hallowed fishing grounds, the Flemish Cap could have been a baseball cap from Flanders. Now, thanks to *The Perfect Storm*, the book or the movie, we know the Flemish Cap is a remote shallow area east of Newfoundland, the last bit of land before Europe. The film folk got that much right. Otherwise, they were blown way off course without knowing it, and if they had hired me as consultant, they wouldn't have gotten me, the critic.

Having read the book and having just seen the movie at the local drive-in, this unexpected meeting with Rob the lobster guy was almost too good to be true. I was still impressed by the lobstering life and kind of hot under the collar about what I considered a glaring cinematic oversight. Needing corroboration from the experts, I pounced. "I'd love to talk car, but I have a much more important question. We both know the ocean and we've been through storms. Tell me, what is the sound you listen for the most in all that racket?"

"The screw," he answered.

"No," I said. "For the sake of the argument, let's forget mechanical stuff. I'm talking about the sound you'll listen for in a rubber dinghy, or on an aircraft carrier."

"Oh," Rob said. "The wind."

"Exactly!" I exclaimed. "Is it only me and you? Or, don't you think anyone who isn't deaf and has lived through a storm would agree?"

I thought so and so did Rob. Yes, we listen for other things—doors coming loose, objects jostling about in lockers, the slosh of rising bilge water, screws, any abnormal above deck sounds. But, without consciously listening for it, the sailor's ear has a default position permanently tuned in to the wind, ready to pick up the subtlest change in pitch. I know for a fact the wind is directly linked to the sea conditions and my emotional state. The louder it squeals, the bigger the knot in my belly, and the rougher and hairier the ride. It's a law of nautical physics. Without wind, there is no storm, no waves, no fear, no nothing. In fact, no wind is called a flat calm, and a flat calm can be outright boring.

This may all seem very obvious to you, but here's a surprise: it isn't for everyone. What were the producers of *The Perfect Storm* thinking when they replaced what must have been an unearthly windy howl with a schmaltzy soundtrack? Yes, it's true. Go see the movie again if you don't believe me. There is no wind noise worth mentioning! I kept waiting for George Clooney to holler for someone to turn up the music, which was being drowned out by *Titanic*-like sounds—plenty of rushing and crashing water, but no wind. Didn't anyone bother to tell them that no storm is perfect without wind?

Does Hollywood think our forefathers rowed over from the old country? Without wind, all of history would have been delayed; it blows through time, across land and sea, in and out of poetry and literature, gentle winds and perfect storms that have generated a lot of other myth and legend. At one time, it was said that whistling softly while sticking a knife into the mast

brought kind winds. Or, if one was French, flogging cabin boys
with their backs pointing in the direction they wanted the wind
to come from was effective. Whistling sometimes called the
wind, but whistling in the wind would bring a gale, and black
cats carried gales in their tails. The Finns once had the short-
lived reputation for being able to control the wind by trapping it
in a bag with three knots; as each knot got undone, the wind
strengthened. Who knows how all these anecdotes were started,
but I find them entertaining, especially since nobody pretends
any of it is true. Only one thing is for certain—the wind had
something to do with all of them.

It's not as if I have any great expectations for Hollywood and
their versions of truth, but that some overpaid nitwit hired
musicians to compose anxiety-making music to heighten the
viewer's agitation as the storm grew stronger is piling artificial
pretense upon pretense, and it is nothing short of ludicrous.
There is no substitution for the unholy racket of the wind when
it comes to building any of the horrible feelings that arise from
a relentlessly accelerating wail of a bagpipe gone berserk. Is it
a coincidence this irritating instrument happens to be a wind
instrument?

The movie's fatal flaw was so unbelievable it was nearly over
before I caught wind of the major missing ingredient, preoccupied as I was by other unrealistic action moments; for example,
every pitching cabin shot showed the same stationary ashtray,
cups and plates on the table. Then, what was that scene all about
when one of the crew clambered out to the end of the wildly
pitching boom with an acetylene torch blazing away? Even the
Towering Inferno couldn't have survived that storm. Come on,
guys! I don't want to take the wind out of your sails, but here's
another law of nature: fire and water never have, nor will they
ever, mix! My kids can tell you that.

I can't remember much else about the movie—in one eye, out
the other. I do remember, however, the relief it was to blame my
squirming on Hollywood's idiotic assumptions about the last

days of the ANDREA GAIL, and that I was able to use some genuinely derisive criticism to resist getting weepy over how they manipulated the tragedy. Forget about tears being jerked when there's a cause to champion, when I've got something to rant about. Call me a windbag, but thousands of years ago, the Greeks invented tragedy at the same time as they came up with gods for every wind direction, gods who were constantly being mentioned. I've even been known to offer libations to Aeolus because superstition must be a kissing cousin to wind for good reason.

As you can see, I have taken it upon myself to speak for the wind. Forget about whistling cabin boys, black cats, and knives in masts. But, I ask, does a movie need to be called *Twister* before the wind gets headlined, or at the very least, acknowledged? It is foolish to trivialize this phenomenon of air moving parallel to earth's surface, and most sailors can't and won't. Some things are bigger than us, and Hollywood. If I had anything to do with the creation of *The Perfect Storm*, the movie, I'd think very hard before ever heading out to sea on a boat, or even buying property along the coast, or in Kansas. As my friend Rob, the lobster boat captain and car salesman said, you can break wind, but you can't ignore it.

PART 4

On Location

Volcano

You've just begun a sailing vacation at a charter base on the south coast of Grenada. One day earlier, you flew in from a major North American city, by way of Puerto Rico, and spent a travel-weary night aboard an unfamiliar and dark boat the charter company left open in anticipation of your arrival after hours. When you opened your eyes this morning, the official charter clock started ticking and carried you off in a frenzy of day-one formalities, provisioning, and boat acquaintanceship. Under the glaring tropical sun, you stowed luggage and supplies, went over the systems, looked at the charts, and a representative briefed you about dangers and recommendations on a proposed itinerary. You've learned the anchorage you need to get to by nightfall is on the southern tip of the next island, Carriacou, thirty-five miles away. There's no time to lose.

You're lucky, and you cast off from the dock by eleven. You unfurl the jib and pull around the southernmost tip, passing one rocky promontory after another before rounding up into the gentler lee of the island. You've seen on the charts that the entire west coast of Grenada has virtually no protected anchorages, other than some meager dents on the coastline with shallower water, and one main ferry, cruise, and cargo ship, harbor town. From this offshore vantage point, as you begin to pass, it all looks pretty good.

If a speed of six knots can be sustained, a reasonable expectation for a forty-something-foot charter sloop, you think you'll be at Tyrrel Bay by 5:30, in plenty of time to anchor and look around before nightfall. But, the winds are irregular, often weak, blocked by the mountains until they spill over and sweep across the flat water in erratic gusts. Six knots would mean running the engine; this is a sailing vacation, you've got a couple hours of fudge time, so you sail, slowly.

Two days ago, you were thousands of miles away, en route to an airport, now here you are, ghosting past emerald mountain peaks hiding in the mist, houses clinging to hillsides below, while the tropical smells of fires and vegetation waft your way. How lucky are you? You play with the main and jib, making sure reef points are set properly, that everything is working while the going is good. There is about eighteen miles worth of coast in the island's lee. Past it, you know you will be pounding upwind into the trades and what could be nicer than taking it easy for now, having lunch, sitting back in the cockpit, pulling out and rereading the pilot book.

That's when you notice something interesting. About five miles north of Grenada and a couple miles east of several rocky islets, you see a detail you recall the chart briefing person mentioned. But, you heard a lot of things. You peer closely at the book's chart sketch, which shows more anecdotal info and less precision than the nautical chart, and you see a five-hundred-foot sounding surrounded by a circle, labeled with the words: Active Underwater Volcano.

Wow! You also see it lies pretty much directly on your path to Carriacou. In the section dealing with passages between Grenada and the islands to its north, the author writes: "cautious sailors might prefer to steer [a course] to avoid the underwater volcano . . . [It] is active and erupted in both 1988 and 1989."

You know the wind honks between the Windward Islands, funneling anywhere from 20-30 knots on your average trade wind day. At the same time, the Atlantic Ocean surges between these bits of former, and potentially current volcanoes, creating

1-2 knot westerly currents. And now there's a volcano confirmed as active in the way. What should you do?

Looking at your watch, you sigh and turn on the engine. No time for dawdling. Quickly, you sail out from under the lee of Grenada's bulk and immediately get hammered rail under waves and wind. You see you're barely making the tip of Carriacou. You round up, using daylight hours that are rapidly becoming more precious to pull in the second reef. You sheet in the flapping cacophony as tightly as possible and start beating in earnest. You watch your destination dance back and forth across the bow, unsure if you will reach it without tacking after all. Whatever happens, you don't want to make landfall after dark in a bay with no navigation lights to guide you in.

"Keep her high, as high as possible," you tell your mates. Sometimes the zigzagging course makes you grab the wheel to stop losing ground for a minute. You keep looking at your watch, the sun, at Carriacou, at some nearby rocks named Kick 'Em Jenny, estimating distances, proximity to volcano, and how narrowly you will miss it. You keep one eye to the water for anything suspicious and wonder what an underwater volcano looks like anyway, bracing yourself for a terrible fright. What was that grayness? That shadow? That weird looking swell? You're as jumpy as the sailboat crashing into breaking waves.

You remember everything you've heard about volcanoes, Krakatoa, the Pacific Ring of Fire, where islands regularly explode in and out of existence. You remember a trip to the Azores, a daylong tour around the island of Faial. Those North Atlantic protrusions were dark and volcanic looking, harsh colors contrasted beautifully with cows grazing in soft green fields separated by hedges of puffy and bright blue hydrangea. You stopped for a drink at a spot overlooking an inland lighthouse that no longer signaled to boats. In the fifties, a volcano had given the lighthouse keeper a view over a new peninsula of ashy fields and cone-shaped wasteland. It happened suddenly, they said, and you know things like earthquakes and volcanoes always happen suddenly.

The bimini shadow is growing longer on the foredeck. Behind, Grenada is a shimmering silhouette under a setting sun. Ahead, Carriacou is a purplish shape stubbornly resisting definition, until you can just begin to discern the characteristic bump of the headland. Behind it, you know a bay is waiting, full of other sailboats anchored on the still waters, people dinghying back and forth to restaurants on shore.

Slowly, but surely, Carriacou gets closer, specific rocks and landscape become visible, and you prepare to heave sighs of relief. It is twilight as you turn on the engine, round the corner and speed up into Tyrrel Bay. Darkness drops over a beach fringed by coconut palms, the anchor hooks, and all you can see is your new next door neighbor, another charter boat with a couple sitting in the cockpit under a light swinging from the boom. They are watching, and as soon as your anchor is set, they call over the water, "How was your trip?"

You wave nonchalantly, walk back toward your cockpit.

"Great," you answer. "Where'd you come from?"

Lake Champlain

Since I'm in Vermont where we do what we want, I've decided it is time for a geography lesson. By virtue of the calling, sailors are generally quite good at geography, placing continents, countries, and remote islands correctly on maps. Oh, sorry—I mean, on *charts*. So, it kind of surprises me when time and again people, including sailors, express amazement at my having chosen to live in a state like Vermont. "Why?" they'll ask. "Where's the water up there?"

Then, maybe a glimmer of a memory triggers some doubt. Or something changes in my expression, because this comment is often followed by a quizzical look and the question: "Or is there? Are you near a lake?"

They're probably remembering scraps of some long forgotten history lesson about Ethan Allen, Benedict Arnold, Fort Ticonderoga and Lake Champlain. Yes, in Vermont, where we do what we want, we have Lake Champlain, which is a respectable 120 miles long and 10 miles wide at its widest, a considerable size that has led some to lobby for its recognition as the sixth Great Lake. We even have a local version of the Loch Ness monster, only this one's called Champ.

Vermonters tend to be proud of the state's celebrated beauty and inland connection to the sea, especially those who live near the lake, and for all the good reasons I discovered after spending a week on it. Island hopping and coastal cruising in different countries around the world ten days at a time for my job, which makes up the bulk of my sailing, hasn't allowed for the intimacy of a lake to cruise within 75 minutes of my home, a completely new frontier.

On our first day out of Burlington, northern Vermont's major city and the charter company's home base, we had 28 miles to go to the first anchorage and little wind. The ladies took turns steering, feeling the wheel, the light air in the sails, catching little puffs and watching the bubbles creep past the boat. We stayed in American waters because this is also an international lake with borders and customs for French-speaking Canada, and in the days that followed, we sailed from Deep Bay and Grand Isle south to Westport. Between the purple Adirondacks of New York and the Green Mountains of Vermont, anchoring in cute little coves and bays surrounded by the cliffs, boulders, hard and softwood forests, and lakefront homes overlooking it all, I read the pilot book and stories yoking local history to the rest of the world.

It is an often-overlooked fact that during the Revolutionary War, several major maritime battles commanded by Benedict Arnold, Ethan Allen, and the Green Mountain Boys were waged on Lake Champlain, with cannon-wielding fleets defending the navigational artery and staving off the Brits assailing the northern border.

In the old days, as far back as the seventeenth century, explorers, trappers and settlers on ships heading up the St. Lawrence River, bound for Quebec and Montreal, were hanging lefts onto the Richelieu River with their canoes. This highway merged with Lake Champlain, Lake George, the Hudson River and points south, with relatively short portage distances between each body of water. Eventually, construction of the inland canal system linked all the seaways, lakes, and rivers together, and shipping and commerce went unrestricted from Montreal to New York City and the Atlantic Ocean, via Lake Champlain and the harbors of coastal Vermont. It is possible to circumnavigate the northeast corner of the United States, and Vermont runs along the westernmost fringe of this loop.

Midweek, I pulled out my notebook full of lists and boat details that was doubling as a log and wrote, *"We've been cruising all day at speeds just under three knots, happy when the log registers changes after the decimal point—1.2 to 1.3 to 2.1—and frowning when it sinks back to 1.6. We're doing the idyllic sailing thing that has inspired so much reflection on the merits of going somewhere slowly, as opposed to the hectic pace of the workaday life that must always be going somewhere fast. I haven't ghosted along at such a slow pace in a very long time."*

I hadn't, nor had I realized how much I missed it. The groups I'd been leading for the previous seven years were geared toward fitting in as much distance and as many sights as comfortable and possible for seven-to-ten-day itineraries. Typically, as soon as the average speed dipped below 3-4 knots, the engine went on, but within the safe and close confines of Lake Champlain, with nothing but a week of anchorages ahead, we were in no hurry. As I listened to the soft gurgling and basked in the relaxed atmosphere, I gazed at clusters of triangular, white sails dotting the lake framed by mountains, a tableau of boats moving imperceptibly against a spectacular backdrop. It wasn't Turkey, Greece, Thailand, Bora Bora, Grenada, or the Riviera. It was Vermont, and it was beautiful.

I'm no lobbyist and will not use this space to seek another title for my state's lake or to convince anyone of Champ's existence since there are several other bigger lakes in North America just as deserving of the title of Great Lake, and who has time for chasing monsters? But one trip on Lake Champlain taught me more about history and a part of life where time can become relative—here, in Vermont, where we can do what we want, and as it turns out, both by land and by sea.

Withdrawal

⁓

The atmosphere aboard the sailing vessel VIRGO reminded me of a movie portraying a hostage situation in its third day, at the point when the victims have begun to lose hope it will soon end. What the next minute will bring is entirely out of the hostage's hands because much bigger powers are holding those cards, and so the meaning of life becomes a waiting game.

As we pounded across the 48-mile-wide distance of open Greek waters between Kythnos in the Cyclades and Hydra in the Saronics, my subdued crew looked as if they were being held hostage by the boat and the wicked meltemi, the prevailing northerlies of the Aegean Sea. Several hours into the trip, I was sitting on the windward side of the cockpit, hypnotized by the southbound procession of whitecaps passing under our keel when a wave splashed across the deck, slapping me to attention and reminding me I was captain, responsible for the boat and my shipmates. I checked in on both and the hostage image was born.

Below decks, Lisa had staked out her position for the duration, curled up behind the saloon table. Bob was wedged between the fridge under the chart table and the island amidships, his head hanging to his chest and his eyes at half-mast as he bobbed with the boat's lurching motion. His wife, Starr, was in their cabin where she had disappeared within minutes of leaving the dock. Sara had retreated to her cabin as well, forced by a limited wardrobe to go where it was warm and relatively dry. Indomitable

Marge, taking a break from cleaning and mothering, was sitting at the unoccupied end of the saloon table gripping her sandwich with one hand, the edge of the table with the other, also staring into nothingness, body swaying back and forth to the VIRGO beat. Out in the cockpit with me, Jim and Lisa sat hunched over, staring at the waves while Walt grimly maintained a firm grip on the wheel, the only guarantee he had against getting sick.

We had left Loutra, a small harbor on the northeast coast of Kythnos at first light, and motored about three miles into the enormous waves deflected off the rocky coastline; before the other two boats in the flotilla passed us, we watched them fly over crests so far that we could check out the antifouling and anodes on the forward halves of both keels. Pounding into 40-knot winds and breaking waves before rounding the northernmost point and being able to head off on a beam reach for the rest of the day was a completely drenching experience, and it didn't set the best of moods for the rest of the passage.

Forty-eight miles with nine people in kind weather makes for conversation, banter, snacking, sunbathing, tranquility, and an activity level entertaining and relaxing enough to let the hours pass painlessly. The passage becomes an extension of life ashore, hours spent winding down from the last island and gearing up for the next while working on the tan. When the forty-eight miles require foul-weather gear, seasick medication, bilge monitoring and pumping and reefed sails, however, despair, churning tummies, and overall discomfort can make the upcoming landfall feel unreal, as if such misery could know no end. This was what I saw among my quiet crew on this blustery crossing.

Nobody was smiling. VIRGO was heeled over with only half the canvas out and still averaging a cool eight knots, yet nobody was shouting ebulliently with heady exhilaration and the thrill of being out there riding the seas. I wasn't smiling either, for another reason. My foul-weather gear may have looked good and professional, but every seam was a sieve and I was soaking wet and freezing cold, wondering if I would be able to recognize the first signs of hypothermia and if I got it, would I still be able to dock the boat later, hold a hot drink, and play some more backgammon?

By now, the sails had been set perfectly, the course was plotted, lines were coiled and tied down, all loose articles were stowed—everything that needed doing had been done and for all of us, the idea of a landfall was sounding pretty good. Waiting for this to happen was the objective. No matter how the situation was reconfigured, our hull speed was 8 knots and we still had to wait for one slow mile after another to pass, 7.5 minutes or 450 seconds at a time. First, Kythnos had to disappear behind us before we could start searching the horizon for the vague and distant outline of Hydra, which would become progressively more defined until lighthouses, stonewalls, homes, terraced gardens, and harbor entrances could be distinguished.

Compared to the current situation, hindsight turned the memories of sleepy Kythnos and the even sleepier harbor of Loutra, which had been closed down for the winter season, into a virtual hotbed of excitement, not to mention the most stable and comfortably level spot on earth. How could anyone ever leave paradise for this, on purpose? The cruising life is about being somewhere, and barring the rare ideal conditions, the getting there part is a necessary evil. I totally understood the sentiments of regret and resignation aboard because they were old friends of mine.

I know well this timeless void between two harbors, neither here nor there, this place that distorts the present, making the promise of the future fall woefully short of the proven security of the past. What I also know is this is a phase. This pathetic attitude is just one stage of the withdrawal we must go through when we set sail, when we choose to be cut off from the comforts of society. Without getting airlifted off the deck (or being helicoptered off Kythnos, like the Swedish flotilla that had been sharing the dock with us) the road to Hydra had to be traveled with more of a risk factor and at a much slower rate than most things we do in these days of high speed communication, transportation, and instant gratification. We are civilization junkies, and it takes time to purge its cluttering effect from the system enough to appreciate the combination of a challenge and the simplicity of getting from here to there at a leisurely pace.

It takes time to be able to accept this necessary evil as a gift, not a punishment, that we aren't really hostages on our boats, regardless of the weather. We have to learn how to be grateful for what this void can offer, how to master the waiting game. It can take days of discomfort, malaise, and a sense that we are missing out on something important until the withdrawal is complete, until 6-8 knots becomes the ideal speed, the ocean the only place to be, and civilization a place full of people who could never understand. The gift comes when we are able to move away from feeling helpless to knowing that being at sea means being free and more in control of our own lives than we can ever be on land.

But, I also know this transformational process is more available to the long-distance sailor I once was, not the island-hopping sort I have become. When the island-hopping conditions become anything less than ideal, though, I am able to revisit something approximating the withdrawal symptoms I remember from longer trips. It is also when I can see how it affects others who are being introduced to this passage from one stage of experience to another, where a landfall becomes not a right, but a reward for personal achievement, whether the crossing is from the Galápagos to Tahiti, or Kythnos to Hydra. Finally, as witnessed by the excited tales that flew about at the end of this revealing day, the reward for suffering from the cold, for getting hammered by wind and waves, or for hanging overboard for hours, was sweetened by the release of all the stories that we had been holding hostage until the waiting was over.

Procrastination

~～⌒

Tahiti was like nothing I had ever seen or experienced before, and I loved it. For five months in 1986, I was anchored in Arue, a tranquil lagoon, waiting out the South Pacific hurricane season. Visually, this dot in the middle of the ocean was stunning: coconut palm-lined beaches punctuated by hibiscus-laden grass huts, luxury hotels, and the occasional troupe of dancing girls; prolific and familiar-looking vegetation blanketed the landscape, enormous leaves exploding from every crack in the contrasting black volcanic rock. Waterfalls cascaded into tumbling rivers, and, with new friends, I sailed, snorkeled, swam, and rowed across the lagoons stretching from headland to headland, while the wildly verdant peaks overlooked it all.

In those days, Arue was home to a small marina with showers, a full-size soccer field for neighborhood kids, and a shed housing native racing pirogues. On the main road leading to town, a take-out Chinese restaurant provided a cheap alternative to the plentiful finer fare that tempted me every time I got off the boat. The islands of French Polynesia are part of France's dwindling collection of colonies, and the combination of Gallic and Polynesian influence creates an exotic blend of cuisine, not to mention plenty of guy watching. The place is synonymous with dream, a dream to behold, a dream to experience. What more could a nineteen-year-old girl ask for?

The camera in my memory pans over this paradise of all that

was beautiful and fun for me. It takes in Arue, lingering on the smiling faces of the friends I made, passing the roaring fires under the woks cooking up my lo mein, to the hibiscus and bougainvillea-lined parking lot where I learned how to drive a stick shift (on a rental). It zooms in on the tabby kitten who became my companion, and then it sweeps back out to the puffy clouds marching west and the sparkling waters stretching beyond the white line of the distant reef. There, in the middle of a turquoise lagoon, I can see VARUNA, my beautiful boat, my home, gracefully swinging at anchor in this panoramic postcard shot, and . . . all of a sudden, the camera screeches to a halt. My internal soundtrack of idyllic and swaying island music stops mid-note and gets replaced by some discordant, experimental stuff from the budgie bin.

What? What happened? What ruined the mood? The boat? No way. I loved my boat. She was a thing of beauty, diminutive, yet regal, all twenty-six of her slender, burgundy feet. No. The interruption comes from my overactive, built-in system of reality checks, this one being a reminder of all the work the sight of VARUNA represented. She was my first home and also my first major responsibility, where I learned how procrastinating too much is never a good idea, especially on a boat where there is no end to the housekeeping. I had saved so many jobs and chores for Tahiti that they were what used up time spent on this island, more than all the dreamy fun and games.

Between New York and French Polynesia, VARUNA and I sailed our 6,000-mile shakedown cruise, through six months of ocean wear and tear. When we started the voyage, VARUNA was a brand-new boat and, by Tahiti, she was overdue for a bit of attention before we could continue plying westward. In reality, on location in Arue, whenever I looked out at VARUNA, I couldn't always see the Tahitian ideal that has been saved on the surface of my memory. I saw, instead, a load of work.

The cockpit floor, which was removable and doubled as engine access (for an engine that was lifted out for a complete overhaul), had to be modified to prevent salt water from seeping in and gnawing away everything. The batteries had to be brought up out of the bilge, contained, and bolted down somewhere in the drier cabin, and a solar panel needed to be purchased and installed to ensure a reliable charging source.

Masthead light bulbs needed replacing, but not before a new solution was found for securing the mast steps to the mast (aluminum mast and screws with stainless-steel steps had created a dynamically corrosive duo, so I tried stainless screws). VARUNA also needed to be hauled out for an antifouling, and something had to be done about the freshwater tanks that were tainting the water they carried. An extra length of anchor rode was waiting to be spliced on to the existing chain, and there were tons of smaller domestic tasks—building an addition to my bunk, fitting a new foam mattress, and sewing new cushion covers, to name a few. The list was there, but it came without the instructions on where and when to start, the thing a procrastinator needs most.

What I knew for sure, and what kept the fire burning under me, was I still had three quarters of the world to go and VARUNA and I had to leave by the beginning of May to keep ahead of hurricane seasons in upcoming oceans. When I first dropped anchor in Tahiti, five months seemed like forever—150 days—which was kind of like thinking oneself rich while holding a wad of one-dollar bills after cashing a paycheck. Mondays, the day when "I could get back to work because the chandlery was closed on Sunday," vaporized, one after another, as fast as one-dollar bills disappear. It took longer than it should have for me to reach an understanding of the concept of time, and how the only way it can be measured is by what we do with it.

In spite of my procrastination, and all the dithering, planning, and discussing the tasks at hand from every imaginable angle, the jobs got done. After the last coat of antifouling was applied, when I finally pulled up anchor and left Tahiti in mid-May, not much later than planned, my memory began the selection process. Because of the work and how great it felt to get it done, the paradise part seemed well earned, and recollections of the time I spent in between jobs, swimming, snorkeling, sailing and hanging out with the friends I made have become even richer in hindsight. This just wouldn't be the case if I had spent five months sunbathing. And so, I need to keep reminding my internal camera of a big cruising truth: work is the reality, and the dream is what you have once the work gets done. Cut.

Greece

My first visit to Greece was an unplanned pit stop. I was heading from the Suez Canal to Malta on a windless Mediterranean Sea and burning up fuel like an SUV. When the gauge needle neared the empty mark, the southern coast of Crete wasn't very far away. My large-scale chart of the Mediterranean showed a little cleft marked by the name "Loutra," just east of the sizable town of Palaiokhora. It seemed like a clear shot with plenty of deep water all around. Sure enough, on the approach, there were no navigational surprises and Loutra ended up being the quaintest cluster of buildings nestled at the foot of some pretty steep Cretan real estate.

After something like a week at sea, I anchored in the light-blue shallow water near a beach covered with young sunbathers and looked around. Umbrellas advertising different brands of ouzo shaded the tables in front of tavernas and rooming houses teeming with bodies—July in Greece.

Having just emerged from the entirely different world that lay on the other side of the Suez Canal, I inflated the dinghy and threw in the diesel jerry cans, eager to do some European people watching. I wasn't disappointed. Plunking myself down at the first table, weather-worn, bleached out and salty, I watched the latest fastidiously maintained fashions parade by, and ordered up a plate of sautéed string beans to satisfy a craving for fresh vegetables. The innkeeper was very chatty, curious about where such a scruffy creature had come from and where I was headed, which led quickly to the fuel question. As it turned out, Loutra's main attraction was that it was only accessible by ferry. No roads led to the cove, therefore, no cars. Obviously, this was a romantic ideal for tourists, but for me it was absurdly inconvenient. No cars meant no fuel, and after a brief respite in this oasis, I motored over to Palaiokhora and filled up there before pointing the bow to Malta.

My two-day Cretan sejour is a blip on the screen of memories of that trip, a reintroduction to a world completely different from the Middle East and Asia I had just left in my wake. Eight years went by before Greece came back onto my radar, and stayed there, when I started working with a sailing school that organized overseas trips. Greece has been a favorite destination for as long as tourism and travel have existed, for good reason. From the get go, I was hooked.

Stepping off the airplane from New York, in Athens, a throng of smokers yelling back and forth and hugging each other surrounded me in a cacophony of sound, smell and energy. So began my relationship with the high passions, the contrasts between beauty and ugliness, and the fierce love of life that is Greece. With this first week-long flotilla, I sailed to Poros, Hydra, Spetsai in the Saronic Islands, and Monemvasia on the Peloponnesian coast. Between the food, the harbors that were central to everything, the people, the Mediterranean mooring challenge, and the weather, I returned home knowing that the surface of something wonderful had been scratched, and I wanted more.

Fortunately, I am not alone. Greece calls a song that others respond to, so for many years, I have been lucky enough to go back with flotillas to revisit the vastness of choice that is available there for the sailor. Making the decision to permanently move aboard and cruise isn't an option immediately available to everyone, including me. Greece offers the occasional sailor one of the best destinations in the world for one- or two-week-long charters because of its different possible itineraries, and variety of islands and anchorages, each with its own distinctive character. I love showing off the place, sharing what I have learned, and being able to still discover something new with every tour.

I had already done several Greek trips when I went back to school and spent a semester exploring the foundations of western literature. It all started with the ancient Greeks, on the mainland, and among the islands of their melting pot nation. Argolis, Sparta, Achaia, Rhodes, Kos—these were all names I recognized from poring over the charts, not just mythological places. I read tragedies that started in Corinth, philosophy that was first explored in the agora of Athens, drama from the Peloponnesus, poetry from Lesbos, and the adventures of Odysseus who wandered all over the map just to get back to his faithful Penelope.

In the Saronic Islands, there is the island of Aigina, named for a nymph who eloped with Zeus. When her father pursued them, Zeus turned himself into a rock, her into the island, where the temple of Athena was built. An island further south in the Saronics, Hydra, shares a name with the nine-headed swamp thing Heracles had to kill as one of his labors. On the passage from Athens to Kea in the Cyclades, boats can pass directly beneath the temple of Poseidon. Dilos, in the Cyclades, still has the ruins of a trading civilization from a time when the island was considered the center of the Mediterranean and Aristotle was proving the earth is round. A stone throw away from Dilos is Rinia, birthplace of Apollo and Artemis. Epidaurus, on the Peloponnesus, has the ancient amphitheatre where, throughout the ages, these stories have been playing on the stage, from Euripides to the performance of the Greek diva, Maria Callas. Further south on the peninsula, there is Monemvasia, a medieval village carved into and perched on a rocky hillside where everything is still functioning, mostly in its original capacity.

In almost every port, the roads wind, intertwine and double back on each other as they lead up from waterfronts, designed to get invaders hopelessly lost in the land that also is home, by no accident, to the most famous Cretan labyrinth.

This is the thing about Greece. Invaders, Odysseus, Theseus, Helen of Troy, and so many other familiar names with stories that still influence us today, are characters who got around by boat, in fiction and reality. For thousands of years, in times when not too many other people dared to confront the unknown, the adventurous and bold Greeks have been sailing the Mediterranean, in between their islands and beyond. Since boats need to park when they get to land, Greece, over millennia, has been uniquely organizing itself and arranging its culture to accommodate sailors and their craft.

Still now, the islands and the mainland are linked together with cruise ships, high-speed ferries, and hydrofoils, and they all need docks. Every single island (if it isn't just a pile of cliffs sheering away from the water too steeply for anything but sheep and goats) has a harbor. And it is a safe harbor with a jetty for tying up to, a substantial breakwater for protection from Aegean winds, fishermen with fresh catches, grocery stores, and tavernas on the waterfront, because sailors have always been a hungry and thirsty lot.

When you step ashore, day after day, you are greeted by the sights everyone recognizes from the postcard and calendar pictures of a land stereotyped by whitewashed homes, blue doorways, temples and donkeys. The ruins and museums that lay everywhere are reminders of a history that documented and instructed the human experience through art and words. The expected is there, alongside perpetually unfinished buildings with rebar sticking out of the walls and roofs, the litter, and the chaos, which, to me, is the beauty of Greece. This contrasting combination makes Greece feel real, an honest marriage of human passions and flaws that can transcend and strip away the veneer of the ages, and still embrace life for what it is today. I know of no better way to visit and participate in the Greek experience than to bridge the centuries by following in the wake of an established tradition of sail. It is a tradition that brought me by chance to my first Greek harbor 15 years ago, to a tourist harbor with no facilities for any transportation but a boat.

Antigua

Many years ago, I spent four months of a year-long cruise anchored in Antigua on the boat my father bought in England. Along with rotating batches of friends and family for help, he and I had sailed her to the Caribbean via the European and African coasts, the Canary Islands, and across to the Windward Islands, and Antigua. Here, we took a break from our cruising schedule while I varnished all the woodwork and was introduced, for the first time, to an alternative use for a boat: racing.

English Harbour is picturesque, and with its protected hurricane hole, historic fort, and numerous boat-related facilities, it is a popular place. There, boats from all around the world surrounded my father's Rival 38, a dependable, fiberglass cutter. Among hundreds of other vessels, ranging from obviously homemade and frumpy curiosities, to sparkling, bright worked-up, mega-yachts, we didn't really stand out, except for the hideous robin's-egg blue color of our hull. As it turned out, we didn't make a splash as a racing boat, either.

The culminating Antiguan experience was our participation in Antigua Race Week. For months leading up to the big event, racing was the hot topic, Antigua was the place to be, and it seemed imperative for many of the itinerant crew people I had met on the waterfront to secure a position on a winning boat. One of them, an English girl who hitched rides on boats from one major harbor to another in search of work and her elusive

West Indian boyfriend, ended up joining us for the race. Since my father had invited her to stay on our boat for most of the four months he had left me down there, Susan probably agreed to participate because of some sense of obligation to him. Otherwise, there was nothing about our entry to woo a fiercely competitive sailor such as her.

My father saw the race more as an opportunity to make a fun farewell to Antigua than a chance to actually win anything, even though we couldn't help entertaining a lot of "wouldn't it be funny if . . . ?" scenarios. Mostly, the promise of evening parties with the yachting set, dances, and barbecues were reason enough to persuade my father to pay the registration fee and to figure out our handicap in the cruising class.

Immediately following completion of the race enrollment formalities, however, my father began to prepare for the 2,000-mile trip home. We filled up lockers with groceries and tanks with water and fuel. Ever-Swiss and ever-practical, this pre-race provisioning was meant to be a head start on the long lines of other boats with plans to leave at the end of the race. That the Caribbean lapped gently at the hull inches above the waterline was of no consequence to our competitiveness. "Wouldn't it be funny," he asked, "if we placed well, even fully loaded?"

Fat chance. A Rival 38 may be a fastish boat, but it's no racing machine, especially with us on board. For the first three mostly windless days, we came in dead last, even behind a tubby, cat-rigged boat. If my memory serves well, we ended up disqualifying ourselves by using the engine on at least two of those days to get in before dark and before all the party food was gone. With the exception of Susan, our crew, which included two friends from New York, my father, and me, was more relaxed than any race participants should ever be. We spent the days admiring the beautiful big racing boats until they left us too far behind, tweaking sails in comical attempts to catch up, talking and enjoying the spectacle around us. We laughed endlessly when one of the friends, a theoretical physicist, tried to make a rum punch with lemon-flavored dishwashing liquid. "But the bottle had a picture of lemons on it," became his refrain.

This unconcerned attitude seemed to frustrate Susan, our only committed racer, as evidenced by her muttering and facial expression, which darkened increasingly with every better-placed friend who waved in passing. No amount of beer, cigarettes, good food, or stupid jokes that we all thought were funny could cheer her up. At some post-race party on some island, amid the ambient chatter about wind speeds, sail settings, heel angles and whatnot, we lost Susan for good to another world. It was a techno-circle that we were completely unequipped to penetrate. On the fourth race day, as we turned on the engine to get to the beach barbecue before the chicken was gone, my father decided that the novelty had worn off. Cruising was more our cup of tea. The next day we would leave early and head directly for St. Maarten.

In the morning, behind a flotilla of boats full of ticking chronometers, we set the sails in the steady trade winds without having to worry about readjusting them soon to round a mark with all sorts of other boats watching. Heading north and away from Antigua, we started our four-hour-long watch routine. The self-steering was engaged as we returned to our books and card games. We resumed the life of planning the next couple of meals, of soaking up the simpler pleasures in the blue world that was coming to us at an average of one mile every twelve minutes.

This was what I enjoyed most about the life cruising had revealed to me, how to give up the mile-a-minute tendency of our culture and to accept a consistently slower pace. With racing I had just seen first-hand how distance and time get broken down to feet and seconds, which totally defeated the purpose of boating to me. It seemed to be little more than a nerve-wracking job of micromanagement with no time for banter, or to read, smell the ocean, stare into the blueness, play idly with feeling the wind from different angles, and watch for wildlife, the things I liked to do.

When I'm hanging out and talking to somebody who has a passion for racing, or when I'm reading a well-written article or book about a race, I can feel attracted to the excitement of a competition. I had loads of fun on the two other officially organized events I participated in since my first race in Antigua. In Vanuatu, I entered my own boat in the Hat Island Race, and won. In Thailand, our charter boat entered the Phangnga-Krabi Race, and came in last. Also, whenever a group of boats leaves one place for another at the same time, there is usually some hint of an informal and undeclared race, a great game, regardless of the outcome, that I've played with others many times over the years.

Still, the sport of racing has never captured my fancy as much as the cruising lifestyle. After years of crossing oceans, following the dots of harbors and islands, I have decided that cruising and racing are so unrelated that comparing them is like saying, "I like red sails more than flying fish." So I won't. Instead I'll just say that ever since my first taste in Antigua, I've always been more drawn to the one that allows for daydreams, lots of daydreams, and the slower pace by which to live them.

Shipping Ashore

As I write, it's 12° below zero outside, and it has been hovering at or near this mark for almost two months. Trees are cracking, pipes are freezing, car doors won't open, and the banks of snow lining the roads don't shrink at all, while firewood piles do. During the month of January, the temperature rose above 30° twice, on the 1st and the 30th. You know it has been wicked cold for a very long time when 20° is warm enough to leave your hat and gloves at home. But, as of yesterday, even 20° feels cold to me because the boys and I just returned from eight much warmer days on Trinidad's little sister island, Tobago.

My father is responsible for this Tobago holiday. It was great fun, and so is my father for having made it possible. As patriarch of the Aebi clan, he arranged a tropical reunion for his family, which has grown exponentially over the years. From his own four offspring have sprung seven grandchildren, and we're pretty spread out geographically. One sister lives in Switzerland, another sister lives in London with her family, our brother lives in upstate New York with his family, and I live in Vermont with my family. We've met up in fits and spurts at different houses over the years, but this greatly expanded version of the Aebis has never spent eight days together, much less in two adjoining houses with swimming pools under banana and coconut palms. This trip also ended up being only my second time on a Caribbean island without a boat, and man, was this perspective on island life ever different, and not just because I was with my crazy family.

As it so happens, the last time I was on an island boat-less was also with my family, when I was thirteen, at a Club Med antidote to civilization in Guadeloupe. I don't remember much about it except for a frantic desire to distance my teenage self from the rest of my embarrassing relatives and staying out of the sun so as to not ruin my punk pallor with a healthy-looking tan. I've matured some since, and in that time many other nearby islands have been visited. On our way down to Tobago, we flew over Guadeloupe, and I showed my first island to my kids, then pointed out Montserrat and its smoking volcano, Les Saintes, Dominica and Martinique. The volcano was cool and elicited some excitement, but the names of the other islands didn't do much for them because they don't have my ingrained bird's eye view of each place that comes from years of poring over charts.

That first adolescent trip to Guadeloupe has been followed by many other sailing touchdowns on links of the Leeward and Windward Island chain. Between the Virgin Islands and Grenada, I've popped in and out of crowded harbor anchorages and idyllic crystal blue lagoons with boats of all sizes and shipmates of all kinds. When I was younger, enjoying the cruising lifestyle was made possible with my family and my father's dime, and as an adult, the avocation became the vocation. Then I began skippering on my own, chartering and working the boats and flotillas that keep bringing me back to the islands because it's the only way I've been able to afford sailing.

After years of paying for my tourism with the associated necessities of analyzing every cloud, dealing with fresh water conservation issues, beach and surf dinghy landings, dinghy dock hangers on, waterfront markets and provisioning, mooring balls, anchorages, reefs, engine problems, dragging anchors, and the harbor sub-culture that exists for the itinerant world of sailors, I found myself on an island with boats as a backdrop rather than being on a boat with island scenery as the backdrop.

There I was, in a house with no less than five showers and six flushing toilets, a dishwasher, a swimming pool, a laundry room, an unlimited water supply, an enormous fridge and a car, the height of land-based ease and convenience (which is nice where the needs of seven children under the age of eleven are concerned). A short walk across a golf course and up the road was a beach where the kids frolicked in the gentle surf, practiced their newly acquired snorkeling skills, or rested in the shade of coconut palms. I sat, watching them play and shout at each other to come see another barracuda, moray eel, or stingray, and knowingly eyed a couple of anchored sailboats rocking gently on the swell.

To the casual observer on land, the motion could appear to be gentle rocking, but I've been there. Below those serene-seeming decks were lockers filled with clattering and rolling objects and doors swinging free of latches and banging into walls (I still have a blackened thumbnail that got caught in the hinge side of an errant door on my last Caribbean sail three months ago). Dishes were sliding across tables during meals, no cup was safe, and balance was constantly being challenged for the sailors aboard. But, if they didn't like it, I also knew how easily they could pick up the anchor and sail to a quieter bay, island, country, or continent on their own time, at any time, and that is precisely why the call of the sea sounds much louder for me than any luxuriously appointed villa ever could. While our front yard was limited to what the immediate environment of our house for the week offered, any bay or harbor on the beautiful island of Tobago (and beyond) was there for these sailors' taking, and the work and inconvenience that earns this freedom is well worth it.

I saw other anchorages during that week, and it was always from the beach. We did boardings and landings with glass-bottom boats and fishing boats taking us out to snorkeling sites and offshore islands. Instead of me standing in the swell and holding the dinghy in position for other people, then jumping in myself, dropping the outboard, and roaring off before we surfed back onto the sand, local skippers helped us aboard. One day, my father took my boys (his eldest grandsons) deep sea fishing, trolling for whatever bit, and now my eleven-year-old has a picture with his first mahi mahi, and I didn't even have to worry about getting it aboard, killing, and cleaning it. We just had to worry about sunscreen and child feeding schedules, and it felt strange to be in my island element, but not really be there in the way I knew best. Without a boat, I felt very much like Nicholas' mahi mahi, a purposeless fish out of water.

The difference wasn't just about the visual aspects of visiting an island by land or sea, but it was also between the degrees of responsibility that come with both approaches. Call me crazy (and I do), but I missed the work. For me, an island experience from the vantage point of a villa could never match in quality the personal satisfaction earned by the effort involved with being there on a boat. In fact, from exposure to the alternatives, I know the degrees of self-accountability and freedom that can be had traveling by sea or land are about as different as the degrees two separate thermometers would show right now in Tobago and Vermont.

PART 5

Words

Bugs

⟡

Once again, it was time to write, and once again, a shortage of ideas had me wandering about the house and property, waiting for the computer screen to fill itself with the perfect words. I did a bunch of chores, tidied, and strolled over to the recently refurbished chicken coop to watch the baby ducks grow and count eggs from the laying hens. Then, it got really hot and I had to retreat to my basement office, the only cool place around. Being forced by nature and deadlines to chain myself to the chair, I scanned the bookshelves lining the walls.

On the shelf directly above my desk, among the reference books, there sits the one book I've owned the longest and consulted the most often. It is *The Ocean Almanac*, by Robert Hendrickson. The subtitle reads: *Being a Copious Compendium on Sea Creatures, Nautical Lore and Legend, Master Mariners, Naval Disasters, and Myriad Mysteries of the Deep.* It has scraps of paper and post-its marking certain pages, most of which are falling away from the bindings. It is water-stained, well-worn and well-loved; it went around the world with me.

Books, in general, can be great companions, and fifteen years ago, crossing oceans by myself on a small boat, they were my sanity. In two-and-a-half years, I read, literally, hundreds of books. The supply was refreshed in harbors along the way with book-trading shelves and other cruising boats carrying more readers. There were a few books I never gave up and stored always within arm's reach. On the shelf above my bunk and next to the shortwave radio sat the dictionary, the thesaurus, some navigational aids pertaining to the area I was currently sailing, a few favorites, and *The Ocean Almanac.*

Of all these books, *The Ocean Almanac* has been the only one to survive triage for many subsequent shelves, kept close at hand and taken for granted for a very long time. But, the idea to do this book report didn't come immediately, as lack of recognition is often the plight of things taken for granted. As usual, I had to arrive at inspiration by a much more circuitous route, one that took me back out to the chicken coop.

I live on an anthill. Millions of ants make holes everywhere, erupting mini-volcanoes of dirt in the lawn, the driveway, and the fields. They also swarm all over the chicken coop, burrowing in the shavings and creating new entrances to their underground universe from there. Watching my very own free-range ant farm, I remembered something I read, that Italian, French, and Spanish people were also watching ants invade their land. A 3700-mile-long ant colony had been just discovered in Europe, the incredibly prolific offspring of some forefathers who immigrated to Spain from Argentina about 80 years ago, or so they think.

Either way, whether they've been there for 80 or 300 years, the ants storming and procreating across Europe probably came from South America on a boat. This must mean that throughout human history, on the 70 seas and 4 oceans, ants have been hitching rides on boats. Before humans, they traveled on logs, and whatnot. It made me wonder where the ancestors of my ants came from. Unless they're native to the Americas, they could have arrived on this hill by way of any of these 70 seas.

When this train of thought led me back from the coop to my desk, weeding some ant-infested flowerbeds along the way, I decided to check how many of these seas I've seen, from land or sea. So, I got out *The Ocean Almanac.* Even though I've traveled a fair bit, the answer is: only 20. But that made me think about the other 50 seas with ports, harbors, and boats that lead to other ports, harbors, and boats full of ants.

My ants all look different: little red ones, big black, medium grays, some larger blacks and reds. They must have a varied history and perhaps even, some of their relatives could have been passengers on that boat to Spain. And, do some of them have the sea running in their veins?

I read the sections surrounding the list of 70 seas and found out that the sea quite literally courses through human veins. A 155-pound body holds just over four gallons of not just water, but salty water, the stuff that flows with blood, feeding the heart, the brain, and everything else. And if all the ice in the world melted, the Empire State building would be 20 stories under water. If this happens, it would be a good time to own a boat, or a log, if you're an ant, unless you're my ants and you already live further above sea level than the twentieth story of the Empire State Building.

Now you see the hold the *Ocean Almanac* has on me. Once started, I got sucked right in. Revisiting the book also always brings back memories of my years on the ocean with it, and how it so often grounded the immensity for me with reassuring words. On slow passages, it was very heartening to be able to read about the world's slowest ship, the British RED ROCK, which took 112 days to make the 950-mile trip across the Coral Sea, one of the 20 seas I know. That put the week or so the crossing took me into a whole other perspective. When I got tired of hauling, hanking, and changing sails, I could still feel sorry for the crew of another British ship, TEMERAIRE, which carried the most sails ever, 5,100 feet, or two tons, of canvas. When the aloneness got to me, I could read about the earliest recorded voyage in 7250 B.C. when the Greeks started trading between the mainland and the island of Melos. From there, the list goes on through the ages to 1984, when the almanac was published, summarizing nautical history, and underscoring how I was actually sailing in very good and plentiful company.

You can flip through the pages to find a list of places to get started in scuba diving, and learn from the following paragraph that more cowboys have drowned trying to ford rivers than have died in gunfights. Here's another factoid that should be interesting for beer drinkers. When he went down half a mile under the surface of the Pacific, the first thing U.S. Admiral R.J. Galanson saw on the ocean floor was a beer can.

Under *Superstitions*, you can find out all the things sailors should never do. Among them, black bags give traveling seamen bad luck; avoid flat-footed people, but if you happen to meet one on the way to the ship, you must speak first; women aboard a ship are bad luck, but naked women aren't; and all seas are purified at the full moon. Clearly, someone thought up this last one back in the days when the seas were cleaner.

Finally, I checked the index for anything on ants. Nothing. But there is one mention of insects. We have classified over 1,000,000 species of insects and only one of them lives on the ocean. All the others, like my ants, find passage on floating things. And aboard all floating things that are boats with readers, a copy of *The Ocean Almanac* should have an accessible berth. It is a good self-teaching tool and an excusable diversion that makes procrastinating less noble pursuits like fixing the head, cleaning the bilge, scraping the keel, or exterminating infestations, much easier. Now, I have to go see if the chickens laid any more eggs.

Jackspeak

I'd like to offer a small challenge to those who like games. Imbedded here are some common, and some not-so-common, words and phrases that may be attributed directly to the evolution of language that took place aboard ships in the Royal British Navy, according to a little gem of a book I found near the Royal Greenwich Observatory in London. At the end of this piece, I will disclose exactly how many choice embellishments and supporting descriptions have been lifted directly from the pages of a definitive source of Royal Navy "Slanguage," but, please, don't skip to the end. Try and see how many you can detect on your own. Some are obvious because they require parenthetical definitions, others aren't, so easy does it.

When we believe everything happens for a reason, a logical step for the curious would be to unearth those reasons. Sometimes, the route is long and winding, but when a treasure is revealed, it makes the whole journey so worth the while. If you were to follow some sort of trail way back in time from the bookstore in Greenwich, London, you would find that the first long-ago question that piqued my curiosity and eventually lured me to this end-of-the-rainbow location went something like: So, *how* could have Columbus thought the Caribbean Islands were India anyway?

Experience with navigation taught me the answer and I have often felt a jack-me-tickler (a sailor who knows everything) pride because I can really understand the gynormous impact time and the location of 0 degrees longitude has had on exploration, discovery, pioneering, and the world as we know it. If it weren't for precision in time and longitude, Rand McNally would be a name in the phonebook; we could be still toeing an uncertain line, finding other continents, states, towns and the corner store by "accident," just like Columbus, who stumbled cluelessly upon a new continent he mistook for a sub-continent on the opposite side of the globe.

How can we cross a line if we don't know where it is? Without the prime meridian, sailors could be still fumbling along muttering, "Yeah, according to the book, I should be there. Mind over matter. As far as a position is concerned, I don't mind, and so, it doesn't matter."

My visit to Greenwich was merely meant to be some more exposure to maritime history, the birth of accuracy in navigation, and some fun with hopping back and forth across the line from one hemisphere to another. The Observatory is in a lovely setting, perched on top of a hill overlooking London, the Royal Naval College, and the Thames, yet my visit ended in a small bookshop nearby, where I hit the jackpot with a book that opened up a whole new tentatively related domain, the world of *Jackspeak*. Mark my words, *The Pusser's Rum Guide to Royal Navy Slanguage*, a dictionary and a gold mine, answered questions I had never even asked. As it turns out, for every person who will try to button my flap when I start rambling on about celestial triangle theory and the prime meridian, there is another who wants more Jackspeak.

"Jack" is a generic name for generations of Royal Navy sailors who coined many unremarkable contributions we all use as speakers of the English language, and many more those of us who try and watch our tongues would never say aloud, much less permit to enter our thoughts without dashing them away on principle. The dictionary's entry for "Jack" itself has many applications and variations as a suffix and a prefix, almost as many as there are derogatory and pejorative entries for Irish, Jews, Blacks, Asians, Maltese, Hispanics, women, homosexuals, and monkeys. If this dictionary and its descriptive contents are representative of true color, I don't think I'm spreading any scuttlebutt by saying those in the Royal Navy responsible for this kind of talk weren't a very enlightened, tolerant, or sensitive crowd, not by a long shot. For example, "boot" is considered an affectionate term for wife, and some hat rack made the acronymic connection between tomatoes in tomato sauce and "tits."

Jackspeak sure appears to offer another perspective on maritime history and navigation with this primitive language that makes the reasons for why the British no longer live high off the hog, wielding the keys to an empire, less hard to fathom. At times, it is quite the task to make head or tail of all the facts balancing shipboard life and a mariner's duty at sea with the mischief of a sailor on shore leave. It takes a dictionary to show how, when these fellows hit the docks, women and booze become a linguistic gruesome twosome that has taken on crocodillapig or lesser-blotched hipporhinoflumboduck proportions.

The authors of this reference tool may come at loggerheads with an etymologist over some of their claims because, cross-checking with Webster's, I have found an error or two. Overall, though, it provides a fair bit of insight into human nature, a life spent traveling the oceans of the world aboard big ships full of menfolk, and a generous hint of the hubris and helioproctosis or proctoheliosis (clue: remember, the sun never set on the British Empire) that felled the former colonial superpower.

To be fair, and because I really am fascinated by the subject, I need to wipe the slate here and quickly honor the British contribution to the maritime world that drew me to Greenwich and the bookstore that birthed this whole word salad in the first place. Globally speaking, for a good chunk of time in the eighteenth century, this was a very important place for the British Empire, her shipping, traders, explorers, and colonizers, who were all waiting for scrambling astronomers and inventors to come up with a dependable form of navigation.

It wasn't incredibly long ago that the age-old pursuit of establishing accuracy in navigation culminated with the publication of the first *Nautical Almanac* in 1763, the invention of a reliable chronometer in 1772, and a final decision was made regarding Greenwich Mean Time and the location of the Prime Meridian, right there in Greenwich, in 1884. Since then, decades worth of ships heading off to other lands have cruised down the Thames, setting their chronometers as the one o'clock black ball dropped from a tower set upon 0° longitude, where time begins and east meets west.

Now, before signing off, let me finish by saying twenty-seven separate Jackspeak entries were used up until this point, and as I mentioned, some are more evident than others. Finally, and coincidentally, today is Friday and according to Jack, Friday is poet's day—for piss-off early, tomorrow's Saturday—so I must go before it all starts looking as if I don't know jack.

Bowline

What's with the term "bowline?" I mean, what's with a word that can be either a knot, or a line tied off the bow, and sometimes a combination of both? The dictionary addles the confusion even more with its assertion a bowline can also be a rope running forward from the middle of a square sail's weather side on a close haul, or a term used as an alternative to sailing close-hauled. "Hey," a captain could quite conceivably order his crew, "tie a bowline on the bitter end of that bow line. We're going to alter course to a bowline!"

Yikes! Saying the word bowline on a boat could be something like yelling "Cookout!" to a throng of cannibals. I think it unfortunate that my favorite application of the word, the bowline knot, and a worthy knot it is, has to share a spelling arrangement, and have its pronunciation be confused, with anything else. The bowline knot deserves to stand apart as the most versatile and beneficial knot on both land and sea. Along with its cousins, the clove and half-hitches, you have a team of Swiss Army knife-like efficiency and they are the only knots I teach.

Of course, other knots are good too. I've used sheet and carrick bends for tying lines of different sizes together. The rolling hitch is really useful for tying a banging halyard down to a stay, and the stopper hitch has kept several anchors from rubbing annoyingly on the bow roller in swelly anchorages. I always make sure that every halyard and sheet on any boat I skipper has figures-of-eight knots stopping the ends on the right side of the blocks and fairleads, and I've been known to employ the reef knot even though the shoelace knot works just as well.

Learning how to do every single situational knot available, however, is great as a hobby, or if one is into macramé, but the despair of ever being able to know them all should never get in the way of learning the two best: the bowline and the hitch. The clove hitch ties down most things, mainly spare lines and fenders to lifelines. The bowline can do everything else.

It's a tricky knot to learn and a trickier knot to teach because we all have different ways to approach things, especially as right- and left-handed people—and, I've watched with great interest other teaching techniques. One woman substituted her own waist for a bollard, another demonstrated the contortions involved in the one-handed method, but my favorite and the one almost everybody has heard, whether or not they use it, is the rabbit story. This rabbit travels into his hole, runs around the tree clockwise, and climbs back out of the hole. Or, he comes out of his hole, walks around the tree in a counterclockwise direction and then goes back into his hole. Or else, he climbs the tree because he forgot carrots are tubers, comes back down, and goes home.

I never remember the direction and the one sure way for me to mess up a bowline tying demonstration is to invoke the rabbit story. The rodent always takes me places I never want to go, namely to the realm of embarrassment, because as a sailing teacher, I'm not supposed to mess up on this venerable knot.

Finally, this brings me to another little known fact handy for storing in a teacher's hat. The word "knot" itself, has multiple meanings. While we know that it is both the term used to quantify speed in nautical miles and the thing we do to lines and ropes, do we know which came first? I do. According to a book I own, in days gone by, speed used to be determined by a line of 120 knots evenly spaced every 51 feet, a length that is equivalent to a nautical mile. Tied to the end of a line was a piece of wood (or a log, hence the term "log") that remains relatively motion-less after it hits the water. Since there are as many knots in the line as there are half-minutes in the hour, however many knots that pass over the stern every half minute, once the log has been jettisoned, equals the speed of the boat in "knots" per hour.

Now, if you spend too much time trying to understand the math behind this, you're liable to get all knotted up. Or, you could get as confused as the poor rabbit who, sick of sailing on a bowline course, clambered down from the main along the bowline, got his foot caught in a bowline, fell tail over ears onto a stray bowline that wasn't attached to any tree, and he never saw his hole again—a situation which could have been avoided if there hadn't been so many bowlines.

Nomenclature

When I teach people to sail, some who have never been on sail-boats before, there are those who immediately see the directness of cause and effect, once they get past the novelty of it all. Some take longer; they need diagrams, notes, practice, and drilling. There's much to learn, from the basic names of things to more abstract navigational concepts, until it all comes together and one can feel knowledgeable. Watching this begin to happen for others as it once did for me is very cool.

I remember when I first started to sail, I took notes, prac-ticed nomenclature, and learned how to differentiate rigs. It seemed very important to know how to tell a cutter from a sloop, a ketch from a yawl, and getting it straight was as hard as re-membering the difference between a large scale and small scale chart. Tell me one more time, which is which? Once I got it, though, it stuck, because really, sailing isn't very complicated, much easier to understand than how each one of these letters keeps appearing on the computer screen whenever I type the corresponding button.

Over the years, I've also seen and admired rigs and hull de-signs in other countries, like feluccas tacking back and forth across the Red Sea and Polynesian pirogues jibing down la-goons, talked with many sailors, and read lots of books. I don't claim to be a huge voice of authority on gadgetry, I'm not very good at brand recognition, yet I've been around and know enough to hold my own in dockside discussions. But, several weeks ago, I made an amazing discovery I would take to the closest dock that isn't frozen in, if it weren't hundreds of miles away. In one area, I'm an utter ignoramus, and I'd bet I'm in excellent company.

We know cruising boats out there, for the most part—the typical ketch, cutter, yawl, schooner, and sloop—are relatively modern inventions, a little over a hundred years old. Sailing vessels as a means for exploration, trade and travel, however, have been in development for thousands of years; on this timeline, cruising, as a lifestyle or for leisure, shows up as a fleck of fiberglass fiber. This wasn't my amazing discovery, though. I have a history of being humbled by history, particularly navigational history.

If you have a thesaurus, and I don't mean the limited kind that comes with your word processing program, go look up "water travel" and see what the tide brings in. It's a good thing to do on a blustery winter day surrounded by a sea of snow being blown about and whipped into whitecaps. It's what you can do in lieu of those other boat environment simulation exercises (another modern diversion) that make too much of a mess in a house.

"Holy jangada," you might exclaim—jangada can be found under the sub-heading "boats." Or, you might also say, "Holy dahabeah, (another kind of boat) there are eight solid pages of small-print words all having to do with water travel!" If you're feeling clever after finding this treasure trove of maritime vocabulary, you might be compelled to test yourself.

Go crazy, but first, let me make a suggestion: start with just the section on sailing vessels. It's bigger than you might think, a one-hundred-and-two-word-long vocabulary test. You could play the alphabet game with this list. Twenty letters are covered, and no sailing vessels have English names that begin with a, e, q, u, v, and z. Without them, it goes from "baggala" to "yawl," via the "xebec," and if you are anything like me, you'll be stopped by "baggala," and from there, a decent test score will go out with the tide.

Did you know there was such a thing as a "bastard schooner?" What is that? Is it fatherless? Or, is it a case of mean-spirited name-calling? While we're on the playground, how would it feel if the owner of a "bully" confused your boat with something called the "bugeye?" Here's an off-the-cuff, quick-witted retort: "Well, your boat looks like a galleass. So there, you old baggala."

The thing about a thesaurus is that topics get broken down into clumps of related terms organized by category. It's a way to find other words for words. It's not like the nautical dictionary, which is cluttered with alphabetical explanations that come in handy when the thesaurus throws a word like "galleass" out at you. Doesn't it make you want to know more? If it does, you can look it up in the *Oxford Companion to the Ships and the Sea*, where you'll find it's a hybrid of a sailing galleon and an oared galley, kind of like one of those boats in period movies that are meant to represent the days before the diesel was invented. Maybe the "ass" part of the word has something to do with oarsmen and where they sit.

Enough of that, you think, and you move on. What else do you or don't you know? You look at anchors. How many of those can there be? Thirty-three? You know the Danforth, the CQR, and the dinghy anchor, but what on earth is a sacred anchor? Or the screw anchor? Could they be related?

Then, your eyes wander over a page to take a look at ropes and rigging, even though nowadays you know all ropes on a boat ought to be called lines. There's a guess-rope and a guess-warp. Guess what? Could it be like a timenoguy, Flemish horse, or the guest-rope? Can they be found near the spirketing or the futtock?

Oh, there's no end to the waterways your reference books can lead you down when boats and boating knowledge is your thing and you are reminded of how much nautical experience and language humans have accumulated. We and our boats are at the end of a long line of culture, geography, and history that all comes together under the great rubric of the sea, and to see what has been assembled on eight thesaurus pages is pretty awesome. It's just a suggestion, but as I have discovered, dropping anchor in this bay of words is a great adventure, a connection to the sailing we love, to its origins in time and place, and a fun way to spend a winter afternoon when sailing is just a dream.

Catalog This

How many times have you heard the old joke comparing sailing to hanging out in a bucking shower stall ripping up hundred-dollar bills, or something like that? I've always had trouble with the idea because I think the amount of money people will spend on a boat depends on how receptive they are to advertising and how much they would spend on a house, kids, car, or any of the clutter that drives our economy. In and of itself, sailing, or cruising as a lifestyle may be much simpler and cheaper than a life ashore, but I have also seen one of the places where anyone who thinks differently may be coming from. This nightmarish place is called the world of the catalog, the home for everything you never knew you wanted or needed until you turned the first glossy page of marketing hell.

I hate catalogs, and even though I periodically cut out mailing labels and send them off in order to be stricken from mailing lists, they still slither back into my life. The other day, I opened one catering to the offshore sailor. I'm taking my boys on a cross-country camping trip and thought a sun shower would come in as handy on the road as it does on a boat—you know, one of those bags that hold several gallons of water with a small hose and nozzle attached. Soon enough, though, the innocence that prompted the shower search was completely eclipsed by disbelief.

If it weren't for a well-honed cynical attitude toward the

towering swells of crap that many of us are seeking to escape when we set sail, I could have been plowed right under. Instead of sucking sounds, snorts of derision accompanied my thumbing through pages worth of gadgetry and innovation that promise to keep us safe "out there."

Listen to this. This particular catalog opens with eleven pages of man overboard equipment. There are reflective tapes, direction finders that pick up signals from personal EPIRB devices, neck-and-vest-mounted flashlights and strobe lights of every candlepower, whistles, bells, horns, rafts designed to haul men overboard back onboard, buoys, alarms, slings, rings, lines, jacklines, harnesses, tethers, life jackets, vests, and personal flotation devices.

I repeat, there are eleven pages of man overboard stuff. Now, I have another question. How many of us personally know of someone falling overboard? Yes, I know it happens, but people also get hit by lightning on golf courses, and one could even get creamed by an errant doorknob from the Mir space station. This catalog would have us believe it happens all too often, and only the foolhardy skipper would leave a dock without an arsenal of pre-emptive safety measures with prices high enough to assure effectiveness. Who's going overboard here? I say, the best piece of equipment is a simple, non-battery-powered harness and some sound advice: guys, if you have to take a leak, attach yourselves to the boat before leaning overboard. Statistical rumor has it most man overboard victims have been found with open zippers.

But, wait. There's more. Next come eighteen pages of computer simulation programs for practicing every imaginable sailing scenario in the comfort of one's study, CD-Roms storing nautical publications and information, and electronic navigational aids, because one can never be too prepared. Then, there are eleven more pages of survival gear and flares, and three pages of medical kits and watermakers. All this is capped by twenty pages of step-by-step cruising guides that can help us navigate

our ways through all the hazards and dangers littering every corner of the globe.

When this is compared to the few remaining pages reserved
for the safe and boring-sounding stuff we *really* need such as actual charts, chartbooks, tables, reference books and navigation
equipment—and mind you, here, too, salesmen of the year have
managed to intersperse many other ways to waste perfectly good
money on perfectly useless reinvented wheels providing employ-
ment for garbagemen of the year—someone who didn't know
better could conclude that sailing is only for suicidal high rollers.
Well, unless, of course, one plans ahead properly and buys all
this safety stuff. But, gosh, how expensive it all gets.

Bilgewater, I say. Don't fall into that trap. The best way to
stay out of the bucking shower stall is to put the catalog in the
recycling pile without opening it, go sailing, and find out what
it's all about and what is needed for your own boat without advice from someone who gets paid to come up with the perfect
sales pitch, preying on and feeding off potential fear.

Now, here's a clincher: the catalog I have been referring to
for this rant sells six different watermakers and related acces-
sories, the cheapest one being manual and going for $562. But,
do they sell anything so practical as a jerry can to store water reserves? No. Do they sell sunshowers to protect us from the un-
interesting, yet very real dangers of dreaded bilge pump clog,
mildewed head, and unpleasant body odor? Nope. Believe me, I
could go on and on, but since I probably won't make Salesgirl of
the Year with this piece, I won't. With this last observation, I rest
my case. You may not agree with my opinion, but at least it's
free.

PART 6

Characters, Kids and Cat

VARUNA and Tim

Boats are bought and sold all the time. Look in any sailing magazine and you will find pages and pages of broker ads and classifieds hawking boats of every price, size, and make. These pages are hard to avoid and every once in a while, a picture will grab my attention, not as a potential buyer, but as a dreamer, and my eyes will linger on it, trying to imagine the story it would tell, if, of course, boats could talk. How many owners has she been through? How many years did each one last? Where did they go together? Why are they splitting up now? Do the consecutive owners keep in touch?

I once sold a boat and her new captain and I have maintained contact. The other day, there was a surprise letter in the mail from him. Tim, who bought VARUNA thirteen years ago, says he is getting ready to "hang up his jockstrap," or, in other words, retire from his job of almost 35 years to sail around the world via both Capes. My first reaction upon reading the news was, "Cool! He's gonna do it!" Then, a flurry of other feelings and memories rushed me in a series of unexpected shapes and forms because of the stories this particular boat could tell, if she could talk.

Fifteen years ago, as an eighteen year old, I left New York with VARUNA, and sailed around the world on my own, via both canals rather than the Capes. I was young, inexperienced, eager to see the world, and bound to the biggest commitment of my

life. I returned to New York two-and-a-half-years older, slightly
more mature, pretty darn experienced, and incredibly relieved I
had made it, knowing I wouldn't have to sail again until I was
good and ready. At the time, I couldn't imagine the day when I
would ever get back on a boat, and when I sold VARUNA to Tim,
I was tearless. The split wasn't heartbreaking; I loved her and always would, but we'd had our fling and the parting of ways was
inevitable.

In the past thirteen years, I've paid tribute to her and the
overall quality of her make, the Contessa. I've given hundreds of
talks accompanied by slides of my elegant burgundy partner
fighting wind and waves, drifting in calms, floating in idyllic anchorages. Coupled with these slides, I have my own selective
line-up of mind pictures that include her witnessing me at my
most fearful and brave, my most shameful and proud, my most
vulnerable and strongest—for ours was a trip of extremes. We
will forever be bonded by the feelings, sensations, and moments
of a first marriage, and thank God she can't talk.

Whenever I thought about Tim and VARUNA embarking on
their own future together, it was in an abstract way, sort of like
how one would think idly about life going on for a former beau.
I knew she was in good hands, and while Tim always meant to
take off with her one day, suddenly now, the reality of it happening made me feel left out.

Never mind that except for the tenth anniversary of my departure from New York when the kids and I joined Tim for a sail
on New Jersey's Absecon Inlet, VARUNA and I have been apart
for years. Never mind that she and Tim have already spent six
times more time together than she and I did. Never mind that
he has been a devoted owner taking more pride and care over her
appearance and integrity than I was ever capable of. This isn't
the point. It's more about a passing sense of finality I never felt
when I sold her. Now, my beau is marrying somebody else and
it's really over. But, I hasten to add, what's over for me is a beginning for Tim and VARUNA, and I am also happy for them.

Now VARUNA will show Tim the world, albeit a colder and stormier one than the one we saw together since he's taking the southern route. I will be thinking of and imagining them in months to come when VARUNA will be Tim's only ally and witness. Winds will clock around, calms will prevail over, the same sun, moon and stars will rise and set above, ahead and behind, and waves will roll under the pair as they did for me. Tim will sit in the nook of the cockpit watching the wake tarry and disperse. He will straddle the cockpit benches and clamber aft to adjust the self-steering lines. He will look up from the same spot on the bunk inside the cabin to check the compass course. He will scramble out on the pitching deck to run up the storm sail, reef the main, juggle the spinnaker pole, and yank on the halyards and up-and-downhauls.

He will find himself head down in the engine compartment, pumping the fuel-lift lever. He will be able to trail his hands in the ocean that is so amazingly close to the cockpit. He will haul the miniature anchor line in far-flung corners of the planet only accessible by boat. He will stand on the shores of these remote anchorages admiring the pretty and tough little vessel making it all possible. Sailing around the world on a 26-foot boat, he may be tossed between feeling like nothing more than a speck in an immense void and master of an awesome universe all of his own. From the vantage point of VARUNA's minuscule, yet comfortably solid deck, Tim will watch this watery world balloon and shrink around him.

Tim knows he is in safe hands. He has a manual of her strengths and weaknesses I never had since they've had a very long courtship supported by a book I wrote with detailed descriptions of our years together. He has also spent a lot of time preparing, planning, and modifying, based on a collection of past experience with VARUNA. The one thing he cannot change, though, is her submarine nature; this will keep them both pretty wet, but never so much as to thoroughly dampen their spirits and enthusiasm. They'll have a blast.

The upcoming trip couldn't happen to a nicer couple. Tim has dreamed about it for years, steadily working toward making it a reality, while VARUNA patiently waited for the big day that would have her chasing horizons again. I am aware of the risk of being sappy with this marriage metaphor, but it is one that is so appropriate to describe the relationships we may have with our boats, especially when they are taking us across oceans. To survive, we become co-dependent on each other, and as with human couples, the intensity of such neediness is hard to forget.

Tim and I have shared a mate and there's symmetry here, with VARUNA in the middle. VARUNA gave me a first taste of life as the better half of our youthful sailing team and she helped sow the seeds of my dreams from late adolescence into adulthood. Tim is beginning his journey with VARUNA at the opposite end of adulthood; they are a mature couple and he is her more experienced second chance. In the fulfillment of Tim's dream, the stories VARUNA will be able to tell will become all the richer, if she could talk. In the meantime, while they're out there, I'll keep looking at the magazines, fabricating histories for pictures of anonymous boats—who still can't talk—in between thoughts of Tim and VARUNA. And, I'll be waiting for the postcards. Bon voyage.

VARUNA and Nicholas

Sailing can be a life of repeated exposure to the synthesis of extremes, making it possible to create a balance and sense of proportion that spills over into so many areas. A child fortunate enough to grow and become conditioned in this environment will never be any the poorer for it. My own youthful education with sailing has created quite the collection of dramatic moments, vivid flashbacks to real life examples of cause and effect, action and reaction. One such experience occurred off the Caribbean island of Dominica and I remember the story in a way that has become part of me.

When I was sixteen, during my first year of cruising, my father and I, and some other family members, were sailing up the island of Dominica's lee side. I was at the wheel, ignorant of the trade wind characteristic of stacking up behind the mountains, periodically gathering force, and then swooping over the top and down onto over-canvassed sailboats. Also unfamiliar with telltale cat's paws that warn the experienced sailor of an increase in wind velocity, I never saw the approaching ferocious gust, and it grabbed PATHFINDER's sails, threw her over on her beam ends, and whitewater rushed over the rails.

With uncommon strength, the wheel spun away from me, but trusting some sort of instinct, I didn't fight to keep her on course. I let the wheel go, and as she was designed to do, the boat rounded up and leveled, sails fluttering. My father was ecstatic

over my reaction, especially since in little over a year, he hoped
to send me off on a circumnavigation. Moments like this only
reinforced his certainty that the sea, a strict and fair disciplinar-
ian, would be the best teacher for me, an ambitionless teen.

Still today, weaving and bobbing, I will automatically seek to
round up into the wind and level out, sails luffing, when hit by
the sudden gust in squalls that blow over us daily in life's stress-
ful situations, be it jobs, houses, schools, boats, airplanes, or cars.
Although, on the surface, predicaments in the stationary Vermont hills where I live are distinctly different and separate from
the predicaments faced in the floating life, especially when it
comes to sure footing, essentially they are the same; life anywhere boils down to our reactions and our accountability to
them.

It is often confusing for me as a grownup, and I wonder what
it will be like for my kids trying to isolate and identify the important stuff as they grow. I love Vermont, my gardens, the
house and a stable community, and there are many good reasons
for being here, but sometimes I wonder if I'm doing the right
thing for my boys by remaining here, plugged into the overload
of civilization and goods that even penetrate this remote hill
country. To make up for it, every once in a while, we do get out
on boats together, living stories that are becoming part of our
own family history, revised and revisioned with every passing
year. The one I like best happened exactly ten years after I left
New York to see the world on my own little boat.

It was May 1995, and Nicholas, four, Sam, one, and I drove
down to Absecon, New Jersey for an anniversary sail on VARUNA.
It was their first time on a boat and the kids explored and got
underfoot as VARUNA's owner, Tim, and I prepared for a sail on
the Absecon Inlet, an inland body of water separated and protected from the Atlantic by a system of fringing sand banks.
Gripping the wooden tiller and falling back into a familiar
seated position with my feet up on the facing cockpit bench, we
heeled over in the breeze and sped along, tacking between reedy

banks and buoys, ignoring the nearby wide expanse of ocean. Tim snapped pictures, we chatted between warnings to the kids who thought the foredeck was the only place to be, and Nicholas repeatedly turned down the opportunity to try his hand at the tiller.

It was a beautiful, salty afternoon until both kids started whining, so we turned back in the direction of the marina. On the way up a narrow marsh inlet, a mud bank hit us and VARUNA stopped. With no potential for a tow in sight, we had to get unstuck alone, and I remembered a trick that comes in handy on small boats. Hanging from the side shrouds, I jumped up and down, leaning my weight as far overboard as I dared, and VARUNA moved a bit, but not enough. Tim left the tiller to join me, and even though the jib pulled in the right direction, every time an inch was gained, the tiller swung and steered us back into the shallows. We needed another set of hands and I called to Nicholas, "Hey, grab onto the tiller and pull it towards you as far as it'll go."

Sensing something was wrong, he refused. "No, Mommy. I can't!"

"Come on, honey," I pleaded. "We *need* you! Nobody else can do this. And we can't eat until we get this boat home."

Mention of food helped him overcome his hesitancy, and he resolutely grabbed the tiller and pulled. Tim and I resumed our jumping and leaning, and slowly but surely VARUNA regained the channel. The subsequent look on Nicholas' face is my sharpest memory of that day, a Kodak moment in his developmental career. It was glowing, he was bursting with pride, and a blossoming earache was completely forgotten. It was all he could talk about and today, four years later, he still remembers the time we ran aground in the Absecon Inlet and he helped to get us unstuck.

Part of becoming a parent has meant facing the awesome responsibility of helping my boys build a solid foundation to prepare them for life. Like many before me, I want the best for my

kids. In lieu of committing to a permanent cruising life, however, I have chosen to provide a balance between the contrasts of
land-locked rural Vermont and examples from the water, from
boats and people in different countries around the world. I can
provide the content, but they will have to write their own stories
and the fun part is watching them unfold.

He may not be a full time sailor, but on one afternoon when
he was four, Nicholas learned something about being part of a
family team confronting a nautical obstacle. We were stuck. We
needed to eat. We had to get unstuck. It was a direct experience
with decision-making and personal responsibility that, because
of the sea, will become a part of his story as it has already become part of mine.

Michel

Once you've sailed around the world by yourself, as a teen-aged female, no less, you will see how often the subject is raised, even twelve years after you've finished the trip. I know I talk about it a lot; there's no shaking such a personal history. It's not that I mind, though. What I'm getting at is how, over the years, different aspects of the adventure have taken on new meaning and relevance to me with every retelling. I give a slide show of full color, freeze-framed moments, and while the audiences hear as much of the story that will fit into one-and-a-half hours, the projector will lead me down a more private memory lane, clicking past one image after another. Interspersed amid a majority of predictably nautical shots, a few with personal relevance always remind me of the connections threading together the years between then and now.

One picture in particular I'd like to mention. At first, the casual observer will see me squatting and reaching out to feed a pinkish pelican, by no means a sensational moment. The picture was taken in Australia and it is used in the section where I briefly touch upon the wildlife there, snugged in as it is between a picture of me petting kangaroos and the trophy shot of a three-foot-long mackerel I caught on the Barrier Reef. In the past year or so, however, I've taken to passing over the random pelican in order to focus on the little man sitting behind it. I met him at the same time I met my future husband, one landfall before Australia on an island in Vanuatu. Immediately taken by his eccentricity, his apparent courage, and the underlying mystery of how and why he ended up on Efate, Michel fascinated me. Anecdotes he had aplenty, yet there seemed to be many unfilled blanks which contributed to his enigmatic character.

Many miles and long before we met, Michel purchased a crappy 20-foot-long plywood daysailer somewhere on the west coast of Africa and souped it up by fiberglassing the wood before crossing the Atlantic. He named it PENELOPE after Odysseus' faithful, long-awaiting, and circumspect wife, and true to her namesake, the boat served Michel well. His misadventures and the people he met between Africa, the Caribbean, South America, and the South Pacific entertained us over many a dinner, but the one I will never forget took place on the Atlantic side of the Panama Canal.

A group of us had been sharing stories about the plague of horrific thunderstorms endemic to the area. I can still remember the fear and sense of helplessness that overwhelmed me as I huddled with my cat, trembling and praying, trying to ignore the thunder booming directly overhead, the torrential rains, and the proximity of the lightning bolts zapping the water around us. We were nothing but sitting ducks as one by one, the thunderheads marched over us, and although I survived unscathed, Michel didn't fare quite as well.

Anchored in a bay with several crewmates crammed aboard the tiny vessel, they were hit square on by one bolt. The thru-hulls popped out, melted, or did whatever thru-hulls do when a boat gets hit by lightning. The fair PENELOPE promptly sank. Only mildly perturbed, Michel and his friends jumped into the water, lifted the ocean-crossing daysailer, carried her to the beach, fixed the thru-hulls, and refloated her so she could continue with Michel across the Pacific to the point where the course of his trip briefly paralleled that of my own voyage.

On the Coral Sea, during the passage from Vanuatu to Australia, there was a blow, a bit of a gale actually, that was an inconvenience to me and nearly provided Michel's comeuppance.

PENELOPE got thrown on her side, her cabin was flooded, major cockpit components were washed overboard, and finally, Michel couldn't just bounce back again. After something like 11,000 miles, in Australia, he abandoned her and signed on with a friend in some cockamamie scheme to smuggle canned tomatoes and red wine into Papua New Guinea.

Before we parted ways, he gave me a hematite necklace and recently, thanks to a power bead craze that is sweeping the nation, I have learned that hematite symbolizes adventure. How perfect. He also gave me a doll, his bizarre looking alter-ego dressed in wide-wale corduroy pants and jacket, sucking on the stem of a corn cob pipe. I am not very inclined to wearing jewelry so the necklace resurfaces rarely. The doll, however, is perched on a dust-friendly shelf in my boys' bedroom. Every time I pass with the vacuum, it stares down at me, and I think about the bearded, scrappy Frenchman and how he has become my model of how often one person's unthinkable may be another's reality.

When we met, there I was, a single-handed, 19-year-old, female circumnavigator sailing an almost new, rugged fiberglass 26-footer with an American Express card and an increasing amount of accolade with every mile laid under the keel. Michel never begrudged me the attention; impressed by what I was doing, he also lavished plenty on me and I don't know if he ever knew how much praise from someone like him meant. I admired him then in person as much as I still admire his memory.

As far as PENELOPE was concerned, Michel knew when to fold, an admirable quality, and undaunted, he continued with other adventures few would attempt. He isn't my only inspiration as I slog through life ashore and at sea, but more and more, seeing the slide of him sitting beside a younger and more innocent me, I realize he has become something of a hero. Michel is the perfect example of one of the many different ways there are to approach a dream, of what we are capable of doing if only we would dare, and we can't be reminded of this often enough.

Effort

During summer vacations, some of us Green Mountain people become hosts to Fresh Air Fund children, an organization that places inner city kids with host families in the country. Shannon has been joining us from Brooklyn for six summers for several weeks at a time, and together with my own twosome of fur-flying squabblers, the three of them have taught me as much about the value of effort as any boat ever has: effort to have it be a good experience for all, effort to remain patient and make sure we never need doctors, effort to keep coming up with entertaining ideas, effort to cook meals that don't provoke a look of disgust, effort to get some sleep.

When Shannon is here, he and my boys expect the level of kid-centered activity to be ratcheted up several notches in order to maximize our time together and I become, for all intents and purposes, a drone, a cooking, cleaning, washing, driving, story-telling drone who looks forward to bedtime from about lunchtime onward every day. This image of myself is a far cry from what I just know I could be, what I have been, balanced before a helm, wind streaming through my hair, commanding a bucking vessel across a frothy sea.

So, several days ago, before the nine-mile hike up and down a mountain that felt like I was killing them, before the goodbye party of 30 we threw for Shannon that felt like it was killing me, I decided it was time to prove my salt to these three kids who had mistaken themselves for royalty and me as their servant. It was time for me to show them who was captain here.

The sailboat is a Precision 14, to be precise. Yes, this fine vessel is my neighbor's trailerable daysailer (currently for sale) that nearly sank the last and first time I used it because of a missing plug issue. That was last year. This year, it barely made it out of winter storage in the barn when I announced my plan to the boys, and when we walked two fields over to pick up the boat, the cockpit was filled with leaves, twigs and wildlife. To assume all the pieces were there, in the sail bag or cockpit, and to drive blithely off, trailer and spider webs in tow, was an enormous leap of faith. But, faith is what I'm all about, faith I could handle my two boys and Shannon on a small sailboat with questionable plugs, faith I could figure out how to back a trailer down a boat ramp without embarrassing us all, faith the day would end happily at the dinner table with more stories to tell, faith it might be a good way to divert the boys from fighting for a nanosecond.

Faith in happy endings is a good thing to cling to when engaged in efforts such as the fourth attempt at backing a trailer straight down a ramp and not off the cement slab. Faith it can only get better is essential when holding a bobbing boat off the rocks while stepping the mast, hanking on the sails, and untangling the rigging just as one of the boys comes for help with a snarled fishing line and a three-pronged hook stuck in a bathing suit. Faith is not a choice when you get all three boys in the boat, point it in the right direction, and all at once, push off, drop the centerboard, mount and lower the rudder, and hope the one boy remembers what you mean when you shout "pull the tiller towards you!" and "pull the jib sheet tight!"

In the middle of the lake, I was ready to start tacking back and forth up to the west end, past the summer camp kids in their Sunfishes, to show my three eager students how to jump from one side of the cockpit to the other, to steer and understand the principle of wind on sails. They were ready for something else.

My boys decided the day was all about jumping overboard and being trolled, and Shannon decided it was about survival. Every time a gust heeled us over with enough momentum to actually pull a kid, Shannon's knuckles turned white and he said he was even more scared than when I let him drive my car to the neighbor's house, which was funny because the opposite was true for me. Oh, it's all a matter of perception, even at the end of an afternoon of sailing on the lake.

We got back to shore. It only took two tries to back down the ramp, the boat got stowed neatly to the tune of more unappreciative bickering about who had been trolled behind for longer and what is and isn't fair about life, which had nothing to do with wind direction or who got to be boat rigger, camp counselor and captain for an hour, or why that same person still had to cook dinner, do the dishes, and write an article that would pay for more fun and games. In the end, with kids and Shannon gone for two days, and several more pages of effortful tales from my fascinating life on paper, I now remember the actual afternoon sail as being the least effort of all.

Brian and Betty

From here, the closest major body of salt water is the North Atlantic Ocean. Its waves crash onto the docks of an East Coast city about 150 miles away where, except for fishermen, lobstermen, and others who work on the water, the boating season is limited to the summer months. The road inland from this foggy, rocky coast passes by blueberry fields, lake resorts, and dairy farms. Then, it winds over several small hilly areas and one major mountain range before it reaches the Connecticut River valley. Here, dirt roads connect forests, fields, neighbors, and villages, and many of them end at hilltop farms surrounded by barns and outbuildings for storing equipment, machinery and sometimes, even cruising boats.

Brian and Betty (their very excellent real names have been changed, as per their request, because they didn't want to be recognized and hunted down by paparazzi) have lived somewhat reclusively in these hills for most of their lives. Before hooting it up with each other, they both had other marriages, children, divorces, gardens to weed, fields to hay. When they started living together many years ago, they started dreaming together, too, beyond all that. They weeded and hayed some more and finished raising all their children while wiring, plumbing, roofing and siding homes to earn what they needed to eventually sail down the river and off to sea.

After messing with and about in smaller boats on local lakes, they found the one that would carry them off into the salty sunset through a classifieds magazine for used boats in Florida. They bought a Luders 36, built by Cheoy Lee, and she needed some work, so they sailed her up the East Coast, to the Hudson River and Lake Champlain. From there, she was trucked on a backhoe flatbed to a tight fit in their barn, close to tools, and woodworking equipment.

A 36-foot boat might not look like much on the water, but put it in a barn that once seemed huge and she'll become massive. For a couple of years, the mast protruded from the back by ten feet and her bow poked out the barn door, pointed in the right direction, ready to go as soon as Brian and Betty were finished rewiring, replumbing, refitting, and replacing interior woodwork. Most importantly, they were beautifying her, because, after all, they had named her MAIA, for Atlas' most beautiful daughter.

We met them when we first moved here, around the same time they brought MAIA up from Florida. They put on our metal roof and helped lay our electricity lines in the ditch leading across the field, under a culvert, and up to the main road. Brian looked like other wiry, bearded guys in baseball caps on land and sea—you know the type. Betty, who, after all their years together still never strayed very far from his side, had long flowing signature hair, braided when they were clambering on rooftops and under crawl spaces, and cascading about her shoulders as they sat around evening campfires sharing stories.

We enjoyed lots of beers and many fires with these two, talking about our cruising and sailing days that had recently ended. As they were uprooting themselves, we were putting down roots, building our own house and family, and we plumbed their knowledge about the ideal size for a good rafter, the best low maintenance treatment for shingles, and other building tips. In return, for every homesteading conversation, we had another about good cruising guides or how many coats of gel paint would last the longest. We told them how we had handled heavy weather sailing and discussed celestial navigation tricks. They even crewed on one of our longer sailboat deliveries from Taiwan to India. We were moving in, they were moving out, and the exchanges of information were smoothing both our waters.

Because I had fielded this question a million times before casting off myself without ever coming up with a satisfying answer for those who couldn't understand, I was tempted to ask them: why are you sailing away? Why not? they answered. Exactly. Obviously. Why not? That's what I once said. Short, sweet, and accurate.

Then, they took it one step further. Why not leave Vermont on November first? Most people in the Northeast could think of at least one good reason to not start a cruise in November. But, one day, because they were finally ready, they opened the barn doors, pulled MAIA out and forged ahead. That first month was their last intentional sail in cold weather since, as Brian says, there's nothing slipperier than snow on fiberglass. Everywhere they stopped, from the launching on Lake Champlain, to hoisting the mast on the Hudson River, to pulling into marinas all the way down to the Chesapeake, docks were yanked ashore as they passed, the last visitors of the season. By January, they had survived their worst nightmare—30° air temperatures, 40° water temperatures, a northwest wind, and a flood tide, all coming together at the entrance to the shallow Chesapeake—and they were in Florida, ready to see what the good dreams were all about for real.

They set sail in 1996. By this time, MAIA had cost them many, many man- and woman-power hours, and about thirty-five thousand dollars. She was simply equipped with a GPS, a sextant, a VHF, a depth sounder, short wave receiver, windmill generator, and the most vital piece of equipment, the Aries self-steering gear. No refrigeration, no computers and sophisticated electronics interfaced together, no yearnings for any of it, and for the next thirty months, this investment in affordable simplicity carried them on a leisurely circumnavigation of the Caribbean.

They sailed the Bahamas, Turks and Caicos, the Dominican Republic, Puerto Rico, all the islands down to Trinidad and Venezuela, the South American coast to Cartagena, and Panama. Somewhere around there, they remember sailing into a five-knot westerly wind with a broken raw water pump for twenty-four hours and ending up five miles behind where they started. From Panama, they sailed to the San Blas Islands, then Providencia, a Colombian island, then Isla Mujeres and Dry Tortugas, back to Tampa.

Leaving MAIA in Florida, they came back to earn more money to continue, full of their own sailing stories. I thought I'd ask them another question thrown my way many times after moving back ashore: what do you know now that you didn't know before you left? Brian discovered he could get used to poor quality beer when that's all there is and Betty realized she had no desire to live in a big house anymore, so they built a small cabin. Of all the stories, and being true thrifty New Englanders, Brian is proudest of the fact they used the engine for only twenty-six hours in fourteen months, for that's the kind of thing people around here like to hear.

Whenever anyone returns from a long journey, another favorite question is: what next? For Brian and Betty, next is to see everything they missed—all the islands they passed over in the Bahamas, Central America, Jamaica, that kind of thing. They're about to fly down to Florida and prepare to head out for a second time, but not before Election Day. First, they want to vote on the outcome that might weigh heavily on the way they will be perceived abroad as Americans. After that, Brian says how long they stay away depends on who wins the election. Bon voyage, again.

Tarzoon

My cat is nineteen years old now, the same age I was when I got him, and he still gets introduced as the cat from the South Pacific who sailed halfway around the world, the replacement for another cat who died. Even though he doesn't look his age, he isn't as goofy as the kitten I picked up in Vanuatu, the little gray ball of fur that kept falling off everything he climbed, earning himself the name of Tarzoon, the buffoon of the jungle. Lots of boats have pets. I've seen other cats, dogs, monkeys, birds, ferrets, snakes, rats, and roaches, to name a few of the domesticated species sailors choose to include as crew, which must mean the inconveniences of pets are outweighed by the pleasures. They were for me.

The story of Tarzoon's life away from his dairy farm birthplace began in my arms and on my lap in the self-contained world of my boat, endless horizons, storms, calms, anchored in harbors with land only accessible by a dinghy until our first marina in the Suez Canal. From Vanuatu to New York, where he stepped ashore for good without looking back, the boat was virtually all he knew. Perhaps it was because he spent the first eighteen months of life on a 26-foot sailboat with a seven-and-a-half foot beam that he never became a very large cat, but what he lacks in size he has made up for with experience and character.

He fell overboard twice, both times in the middle of the

Indian Ocean. The first time, I saw it happen. We were heeled
over, beating, and he slipped off the sprayhood, and I was able
to turn the boat around in time to save him. The second time, I
never knew a thing until the unbecomingly wet kitty woke me
in the middle of a flat calm night, shaking water all over me and
clamoring for a snack.

When the going was good, we would be visiting a country
where I could find cat food. When times were lean, he ate rice,
tomato paste, and tuna stews with me. We also ate other things
straight from cans he liked: asparagus, sardines, wieners, soups.
For a cat, he had a very open mind about food without abandoning his essential cattiness. He maintained a constant deck
watch for stranded flying fish and squid that supplemented his
dietary needs very nicely. Once, in the middle of the North Atlantic, he even caught and heartlessly devoured an exhausted and
unsuspecting canary.

I have a picture of him encountering his first bird on the
Arafura Sea, a largish, gray, ocean type that landed on the solar
panel attached to the stern pulpit. Tarzoon was of toddler age, in
cat years, and like a toddler in a toy store, there was no contain-
ing him. As we were screaming downwind at the time, the main
boomed out with a preventer and the jib all poled out on the opposite side, I knew that if he jumped up onto the solar panel, he
would be history. One bump from a wave and he would bobsled
right down that chute and there was so way I could drop all the
sails and turn around to get him. So, I admit it. As corny as it
sounds, I put him into in a little candy-striped harness I bought
in New York that was meant for a yippy miniature dog. I cleated
it off in the cockpit, got out the camera, and watched.

There wasn't much comedy out there on the ocean and this
moment looms large as one of the best. Tarzoon crept closer to
this winged wonder ever so cautiously, then he sprang onto the
panel. The bird turned, casually looked right at him and lunged,
pecking him in the face. Tarzoon yowled, jumped down, legs
splayed, and made a beeline through the companionway, only to

be pulled up short by the harness. I unleashed him and didn't have to worry about the intrepid hunter anymore that night. Until the next morning, when the visitor left to find some other cockpit free of bird droppings, Tarzoon cowered and stuck close to me with periodic checks from a distance.

He ventured outside once the deck was clear of all traces, which happened soon after the invader flew away because the cockpit also contained the kitty litter. Underneath the tiller, there was a box filled daily with fresh sawdust collected from woodworking shops in different countries and stored in water-proof sailbags. Often, the litter would get dumped on by waves, and my clothes, books, boxes of vegetables and ultimately me, would suffer the consequences. Cats can be picky about where they go and nothing is a better substitute for wet litter than a pile of clean, dry clothes.

This was a major bone of contention between us—me trying to keep the litter dry, and he being too picky and not using it regularly. Sometimes, in stormy weather, the box would be brought inside, a condition barely more bearable than smelly clothes, es-pecially when it was sawdust. Apart from maintaining a sem-blance of dryness, litter quality also had to be addressed and there were different kinds; shavings were best because actual sawdust travels too well. I once made the mistake of getting a bag of teak sawdust, and not only did it get tracked everywhere, but the tropical wood bled a rich dark stain that colored the cockpit, adding to the daily chores a new one that involved a lot of scrubbing. The toilet-training problem was a considerable one that marred the otherwise perfect relationship, and yet, I put up with it, almost happily.

For a young girl sailing alone on the ocean, there was no bet-ter companion than Tarzoon. We had our adventures, but Tar-zoon's final and crowning nautical achievement came at the end of our trip, the night we arrived in New York Harbor. Upon making landfall, I tied up at the Coast Guard station dock in Sandy Hook, New Jersey, for several hours before heading to the city in the morning. While I was ashore, Tarzoon disappeared and the triumph of my return to New York was thoroughly squelched by his absence. The next day, I drove to Sandy Hook and paced the whole spit of land, calling for him, puzzled and heartbroken. I wept because I had shared so many of my memories and dreams with him and he wasn't going to be there to live them with me. Worst of all, I wasn't going to fulfill my promise to provide him with a house to lord over with high ceilings and flat wood floors, and yards, fields, and forests to prowl.

Then again, yes he would. One week later, there was a call from the Coast Guard. A cutter that had been tied up to the dock on the night I arrived had just pulled back in after a tour of duty. When the engines were cut, they said, distinct meows were heard issuing forth from behind a wall of instruments, but the cat wouldn't come out. Wild with excitement, I floored it to Sandy Hook, and at the sound of my voice, Tarzoon burst through a hole and leapt into my arms. Since then, although the sea hasn't let me go that easily, he has never been on board a boat again, and I think he likes it that way.

PART 7

Bearings

Intuition

I often get letters from complete strangers, people who have read my book, or an article, and were inspired to write. Sometimes, they will reciprocate and share a little bit of themselves with me. A few months ago, an e-mail came in from a high school girl in Canada. She felt different, she said. She wasn't like her siblings and friends who were taking the traditional route that led from high school to college and then a career. She wished to do something else. She wanted to leave her small town, take time off to travel, to see the world, to learn about other ways of life and cultures. Did I have any advice or suggestions about going sailing, finding a good crew position, and taking off?

Yes, I do. Typically, in the past, I've suggested a trip to the Canary Islands in December, Gibraltar in September, the Panama Canal in May, or Antigua in April. Working the crowded docks in any of these strategic places can be the first step to a crew position and a sailing voyage. But now, I have a more urgent and vital bit of advice to offer her, and anyone else who wants to listen.

My story may have inspired this girl to see the world, but a book I read recently inspired me to head straight for the most important rule of thumb in sailing related job-seeking. In addition to providing a geographical list of cruising bottlenecks, I warned her to look well before she leaped aboard any ship and above all, to pay good attention to her intuition. Listening very carefully to doubts about the captain and crew of a prospective boat is the most reliable way to make or break the quality of the whole adventure.

The book that made such an impression on me is titled *Untamed Seas* by Deborah Scaling Kiley and Meg Noonan. As a review on the jacket cover recommends, it's a book to read while "only on dry land." If there is any better reminder of the value of our intuition and the price we could pay for ignoring it once the docklines have been cast off, I haven't heard about it yet.

Here is a woman who has already sailed quite extensively, across oceans and with all kinds of crews, who finds herself at a dead end in Maine, desperate to head south to pick up some more sailing work. She engages with a boat named TRASHMAN (warning #1: contrary to some claims, there is a lot in a name) with an alcoholic, irresponsible and sloppy skipper (warning #2: piles of dirty dishes and other filth on a boat is lousy seamanship) who needs help to get to Florida. Aside from reservations about the skipper, the rest of the deal works for her. Any mess can be cleaned up, and in spite of the awful name, the boat seems sound enough, and it's going in Kiley's desired direction.

So they head south, stopping to pick up the other half of the skipper's dysfunctional relationship, and in Annapolis, two more guys board to help on the offshore passage outside Cape Hatteras. One is an old friend of Kiley's, the good guy, and the other is a disagreeable blowhard who, everyone insists, is a great sailor that just happens to have a bad attitude. This would be warning #3. As Bob Bitchin claims so adamantly, the difference between an ordeal and an adventure is all about attitude. By way of a couple of bad choices, bad leadership, bad weather, bad social and team-work skills, and a lot of bad attitude, TRASHMAN goes down, and five people are left with just the clothes on their backs and the dinghy in a nasty storm.

Kiley takes the reader along for a nightmarish ride, from holding on for life under the dinghy, to getting into the dinghy, then sitting in the dinghy with urine and seaweed, then laying in the dinghy with the stench of dying people, then crying in the dinghy as two of the others deliriously swim away for cigarettes, a drink, and death. Five days after the sinking, she and one other person are rescued, and twelve years later, Kiley sits down to relive the horror and pen this cautionary tale for us.

I had brought this book along for the airplane ride to a Grenadines Share the Sail trip. It wasn't the best choice of material to read the night before boarding a questionable charter boat with eight complete strangers. I stayed up way past my bedtime, turning the pages with the same uneasy bellyache I used to stay up late as an adolescent reading Stephen King's books. For the first few days among the Caribbean Islands, the bellyache lingered, and it was hard to stop my imagination from revisiting a world of extreme helplessness and huge waves. I'd feel the rushing sounds of water pouring into places where water has no business. I'd hear shrieking wind, the bubbling, gurgling, hissing sounds—sounds that sink hearts and boats. It was very visceral and creepy, all the more so for knowing how, to varying degrees, Kiley's experience could happen to any of us.

Even barring a disaster, being with the wrong shipmates will cast a pall over the whole pleasure of living aboard, sailing, and exploring. I know this from my own experiences with less than ideal shipmates. Underway, so much time is spent in close quarters that it really is unpleasant when people don't get along. Thousands of former couples and acquaintances can testify to this, too. We are all different and a boat is one place where personalities will clash pretty fast. Unfortunately, the best hedge against this is intuition, and since this feeling comes from the heart and gut, without any bells and whistles, it is all too easy to ignore when it is threatening a dream about to come true.

Being aware of an intuition is one thing; following it is another. Kiley wouldn't have such a disturbing story if she had acted upon her instinct regarding the skipper and crew. But, how do you do that before it becomes hindsight? If your greatest desire is to feel a rolling deck underfoot, to watch white sails billowing, and to heed the call of faraway islands and cultures, what do you do when opportunity knocks?

If you're in the cockpit of a boat straining at her docklines, talking with a skipper who is nodding and welcoming you on board, will you fling the door wide open and let this opportunity rush in, or will you peer out the peephole first and examine it critically? If you have a weird feeling about the skipper, or the boat, will you brush it aside in the excitement of the moment, or will you pay attention and choose to wait for something that feels better? It's good to think about what you would do in such a situation before actually being caught up in one.

Kiley's book has reminded me again of the most important consideration before embarking on any sea voyage as captain or crew. Listening to or ignoring intuition is a pivotal decision; once taken, it is a tack that will affect the course of everything else that follows.

Cashola

Traveling isn't free. Never was, never will be. While this may not be a source of serious concern for royalty, many of us do have to take the cost of things into consideration, from the actual financial restrictions determining a boat purchase, to making a choice between olive or vegetable oil when we provision that boat and take off. Then, the boats demand repairs and maintenance, the engines and stoves require fuel, and the humans need to eat. Once underway on any extended voyage, except for the time spent at sea and on desert islands, even if one manages to get by on the cheap, on some level, the money subject will persist to rear its ugly, toothy, head, and mostly, these hungry maws prefer cash. This is one of the few things I know for sure, and nowadays, access to bank accounts that don't charge interest payments, as do credit card cash advances, has never been easier. ATMs have been installed worldwide, and in most countries that don't rely on the black market, they also give the best exchange rates for local currency.

In recent years, the world of banking has made it so much easier for the world of merchants by eliminating oodles of paperwork, authorizations, and bureaucratic aggravations that used to plague the world of shoppers. The only caveat for the unseasoned, ATM card-holding traveler is to make sure the PIN code is numerical, no letters. I can remember two separate occasions, sitting at a cafe in Ibiza and in a market in Singapore, trying to reconstruct a bank machine keypad on paper to figure out the numerical equivalent for the letters in "tarzan." In Singapore, I succeeded in rendering my account inaccessible because of all the suspicious-looking attempts to get at my money, and this little episode made me wise up and get a number.

Ease of access to cash is part of pretty recent history, only several years old. Not very long ago, other means were used that weren't so convenient which meant, in order for money to last longer, we carried more around and worried more about it being stolen or lost. No matter how it is gotten, though, for every single way there is to acquire money, there is an endless procession of ways to get rid of it, and as I learned, this is an area where truth can be stranger than fiction.

Back in the late eighties, way before the ATM was used worldwide, back when I had my own extended cruising experience, accessing cash in far-flung islands and countries played a big part in the adventure. Even though I wouldn't say no to an offer, I promise I have never received a cent for saying this: I planned my landfalls over charts, the amount of reefs that had to be navigated, and a listing of strategically placed American Express agents in main harbors all around the world. I didn't leave home without that green card. American Express also came in handy as a fixed address that would hold traveling cardmember mail. Because it provided financial security and a reliable place for me to pick up piles of letters and packages from home, at least one major corporation has secured a warmish spot in this cynical heart.

The cash advance limit was one thousand dollars, issued in travelers checks, or actual greenbacks, depending on the country, and in between kitty replenishments, I had to stash it somewhere safe. Before I left on the trip, my dad had given me what is called a stash can, a can with a base that unscrews to reveal a hollow bottom. These cans may be disguised as any one of several popular brands of products and mine was WD-40; it looked just like the real thing. It lived in the locker with other lubricants and fix-it stuff, next to the empty hand-grenade I carried to trick and drive away potential pirates. I wasn't so sure about the grenade's effectiveness, nor did I ever have to test it, but I just knew if there was a better way to hide the family jewels than in a can of WD-40, it still hadn't been invented. This confidence in such clever trickery lasted until the day when the obvious flaw became clear in the unforgettable way flaws in perfection tend to show up.

The day dawned in the beautiful bay of Atuona, on the Marquesan Island of Hiva Oa. This was where I had my first real introduction to the tropical splendor of the South Pacific, and it came after sailing almost 4,000 miles with no engine. Several days out of the Bay of Panama, old unreliable had conked out and my tinkering abilities fell way short of any real understanding of a diesel engine, much less any real repair. In the absence of an engine, I had become a good sailor, but not good enough, I thought, to get through the Tuamotu Islands, a string of reefy, low-lying, atolls strewn between me and my next landfall, Tahiti.

I had a friend on another boat, a Frenchman with a Gallic self-assuredness that outweighed his modest knowledge of mechanics, and he came aboard with great fanfare, waving me off to go do some woman's work—maybe shop, get my nails done, whatever it took to get me out from between a man and an engine. Since this isn't the kind of place I enjoy frequenting, I took off. I don't have any nails to get done, so maybe I shopped for food, and when I returned to my boat several hours later, I was greeted by sweaty impatience and the declaration I would have no engine until Tahiti.

Okay, then. I believed him and prepared myself to become an even better sailor by working through anchoring and harbor maneuvers in my head whenever nothing better was going on in there, which was rather often. The farthest thing from my thoughts was how I would be regretting the hours I had left my engine in the hands of somebody else. Several days later, the time came to provision for the week-long trip south to Tahiti, and I reached into the locker for my can of WD-40. It wasn't in its place! It wasn't anywhere else, either.

Feeling a bit panicky because I was penniless, and uncomfortable because my stash can had disappeared and a stimulated imagination can have a field day with such mysteries, I rowed over to the Frenchman's boat and he provided me with a shock even a charming accent couldn't soften.

"Zut, you keep your money in a can of WD-40? *Impossible.* Only zee Amereecaine could zink of so stupid ideas!"

Yeah, well go right ahead and blame the fact you threw what you thought was an empty can of WD-40 overboard on the Americans and their dumb ideas, you blustering litterbug. That's what he did, no kidding. And, no amount of scouring the shoreline turned up that can ever again. Nothing could have felt more gone than that four-hundred-dollar can, except for the several hours when I should have never left my boat. To add insult to injury, years later, my dad kept insisting I had made up the story to cover a frivolous spending spree, because it's just too absurd.

Absurd it is, yet it's the honest truth. *Zut, alors!* I could never dream up such a goofy tale of human error. Nowadays, though, I think the lost four hundred dollars were a well-spent travel expense. In return, I got a story that would have a hard time being matched by one from the computer efficiency of an ATM driven world, where my next best story is about confusing code letters and numbers.

Provisioning

Planning what you will eat, buying it, and then preparing and consuming it underway, is a big part of sailing. Whether you are planning day-long hops between harbors and islands, or a month-long jump between continents, food fun will contribute enormously to the quality of life aboard. Let's face it. Unless mechanical problems and weather are demanding all your attention, out there you'll find yourself with the kind of time on your hands that, for many of us, will become the hours spent thinking about the next meal.

So, what should a provisioning list look like? The answer is simple. Look in your cupboards and see what you like. One man's beef Wellington is another man's Spam. As far as specific foods go, there really can't be any hard, fast, across-the-board rules about provisioning. Not specifically. Somebody else's list can help you remember things like matches, shish kebab sticks, and a good cookbook, but mostly, what we choose to put in our own mouths is a decision we have to make for ourselves.

The extensively outfitted cruiser with desalinators, freezers, microwaves, and refrigerators has a completely different menu and list of provisioning needs from the cruiser restricted to an icebox, holding tanks for water, and a regular stove and oven. The vegetarian and the carnivore will never see eye to eye. The low carb boat will jog away from those who love baked bread and potatoes. The family with young children needs a whole other range of foods from the cruising couple. Then, what about ethnic or religious needs? There can be no one definitive list for everyone.

But, here is one guiding principle to remember as you wheel those carts down the grocery store aisles and decide what to stow on board: your diet habits will not change as you step from the dock to the deck. If you like corn chips, you can't force a fondness for banana chips by refusing to bring corn chips on board. In fact, it is possible you will come to resent the very nerve of a banana chip trying to replace the corn chip. I made this mistake once, and eighteen years later, dried beans still annoy me.

I was preparing for a big voyage from New York to Bermuda and beyond. I had a lot of fun provisioning for everything I thought I would need, and for everything I thought I wouldn't be able to find outside of the country. I made a long list and based it on one resolution: I was going to eat healthy food out there. I was looking ahead to plenty of sea time, where new and good eating habits could be formed. Forget about sweets, canned foods, fats, and calories. The new me would be indulging in unprocessed grains, unrefined sugars, steamed foods, and tasty wholesome snacks. Yummy!

So, I cruised the aisles of Chinatown and stocked up on dried bean curd, long-life soy milk, dried mushrooms, shrimp, soup mixes, and condiments to jazz up elaborate meal plans. Then, I took the health food store by storm, loading carts with whole grain flour, brown rice, long-life tofu, herbal teas, beans, granola, raisins, twigs, berries, and nuts. All this I packed into airtight and labeled plastic containers and lined them up neatly in the lockers next to boxes of carob cookies and Ryvita-type crackers. In the event of occasional bad weather, I went to the regular supermarket and along with the last minute purchases of fresh perishables, I bought emergency rations of canned tomato sauces, veggies, fruits, stews and soups, and some biscuits, salted crackers, cookies, and chocolate.

I had already sailed long distances and should have known

better. But I was young, an eighteen-year-old idealist who had more than one lesson about the harsh reality of being human waiting to be learned. Now, I almost envy the naïveté, how I'd actually believed the sea would be the perfect environment to deprive myself of what I really liked, a place where a whole new me could be created, because, wait, there's more. On top of all the healthy food, I had every intention to stop smoking out there, where no corner stores lurked to lead me astray.

Somewhere around day nine, bobbing on a swell between New York and Bermuda, you could have found me gobbling down minestrone soup, straight from the can. Then, you would have been horrified to see me chase it with canned asparagus dripping with globs of mayonnaise to stave off the horrible nicotine cravings. All the fresh fruits and veggies were almost finished, the chocolate was gone, the salty cracker supply was dwindling, and all the healthy grains and beans remained untouched. Home made split pea soup? Ha! Let me see if I can find one more can of Campbells, all condensed and salty and creamy. Mmmmm. And, the first thing I did upon making my Bermuda landfall was bum a long anticipated cigarette from a sailor on another boat.

For two and a half years, I sailed this floating health food store around the world, and the neatly arranged plastic containers filled with grains and beans were touched during later provisioning sorties, only to be pushed further back to make room for cans of Dinty Moore. In French Polynesia, I discovered French canned goods, which are a cut above everything else, and I ate thousands of crackers smeared with spicy mustard, and hundreds of wedges of the savory, yet entirely artificial and processed Laughing Cow cheese spreads.

My favorite meals out there, when and if I bothered to cook, were prepared in the pressure cooker after my growling belly had spent hours looking forward to minimal preparation time. Either I chopped up a pile of whatever fresh vegetables I still had on board, steaming and smothering them in canned butter and garlic, or I threw together some fast-cooking white rice, tomato sauce, spices, garlic, and tuna or corned beef for a stew. Every so often, usually in periods of sustained calm, I'd be overcome by a creative urge. Once I baked a chocolate cake stovetop in the pressure cooker, and on other special occasions, such as birthdays, I made crepes with jam. I also liked to try out different herbal arrangements on popcorn.

This is what I have learned: the sea is no place to force new eating and living habits. If they come to you naturally, that's great. But, forcing the changes by deliberately crossing them off a provisioning list while they are still available is asking for trouble later. This is especially true if you are also provisioning for other people. If your shipmates love peanut butter, but you don't, and what's more, you think it is terribly unhealthy and they'd be better off without it, think again. As the one responsible for the provisioning, you'll be better off if you can point out the peanut butter location, or the white bread, or the meat, or the candy, or the diet soda . . . Why ruin the fun in food? Trust me. Out there, the idea that changes in habits can be forced through deliberate deprivation amounts to not much more than the hill of untouched beans I poured out of those containers long after my voyage ended.

Tides

One summer, I drove to the West Coast with my two sons. We traveled from Bellingham down to the Olympic Peninsula, and messed around in the area, crossing islands, bridges, and tidal flats. They played with stranded fish and anemones in tide pools, gathered shells and oysters before the water came back in, and watched fishermen walking across mud to pick up and reset their nets without boats. The boys observed docks lifting and dropping on the sea that poured in and out around the land we navigated, a land surrounded by boats that sat on the ground as often as they swung at anchor, part of a natural cycle as regular as Old Faithful. They watched as land contours shifted, appearing, disappearing, and appearing again. By their puzzled looks, I knew what was coming. It was inevitable they would ask me how the tide works and I wasn't looking forward to them discovering that I, their nautical mother, know very little about tides.

The question finally came in the company of a sailing friend we were visiting and as I hesitated, she jumped in. "The moon and the sun do it," she said. "They pull the ocean up and away from land and let it go again."

I could have let the explanation go at that because it's the general opinion shared by most books, including my encyclopedia, but I couldn't keep my mouth shut. "It's not that simple," I said. "If that were the case, tides would be the same everywhere, even in lakes and seas, which isn't the case at all. Tidal ranges are vastly different even in places that are geographically close."

You see, I've given this some thought. Up and down the East Coast alone, different areas march to different tidal rhythms with mercurial leaps and drops in ranges within relatively small areas. Why does the current in a channel off the island of Euboea reverse itself fourteen times a day in the Mediterranean, a body of water that has virtually no tide at all? It is even rumored that Aristotle drowned himself over the Euboean mystery because, apparently, life without a reason for the current wasn't a life worth living. How can we reconcile the comparatively insignificant tide of the Caribbean which is wide open to the Atlantic Ocean with the simultaneous fifty-seven-foot tides in Nova Scotia's Bay of Fundy and incoming tides that can outrun a galloping horse in St. Malo, France? There are more exceptions than rules when it comes to tides and, while it has never made me feel suicidal, I don't know how I managed to get this far without any definitive understanding on the phenomenon, but I have.

What do you do, then, when you can't come up with a comprehensive answer? Diversions always work for me. When it concerns the kids (and most grownups, too), stories will eclipse long-winded, incomplete, and dry explanations any day and I had two tide-related tales to whip out from under my sailor's cap. So, I told my boys and friend the one that revealed to me for the first time just how complex tides can be.

The Panama Canal cuts through Central America, linking the Caribbean to the Pacific Ocean; only sixty miles of land and a small mountain range separate the two great bodies of water. When a boat pulls in to Panama from the Caribbean, where tides are never an issue, it arrives in tideless mode. I mean, in Colón, there is a small tide, but nothing worth consulting tables and making elaborate dockline arrangements or anchor-rode calculations over.

My 26-foot boat drew four feet and, several days after tran-

siting the Canal, my first anchorage in the Pacific was off the island of Taboga where the water was sufficiently deep that with
enough rode, my boat was fine in the fifteen-foot tide. It wasn't
until I moved to Panama City and anchored off the Balboa
Yacht Club that the extent of this tide and the havoc it could
wreak on my world became evident.

The anchor was set about one thousand feet offshore, a distance determined to be sufficient because it was as far as I wanted
to row in the oppressive heat with a dinghy full of provisions,
and it was in twenty feet of water. I figured my boat was safe.
That evening, I went to another boat for dinner and it was when
the rocking got so bad dishes wouldn't stay on the table that we
realized something was wrong.

My boat, the boat I was on, and another boat were caught in
the midst of a line of rollers sweeping toward the beach. Since
the land shelved so gradually out to sea, as the water receded, the
ocean swell that gently rocked us upon our high-tide arrival
stacked up in the ever more shallow water. I had counted on
somewhere between one and two feet of clearance under the hull
at low tide, and I got it. What I hadn't counted on was the shelving bottom that tripped the gentle swells and turned them into
nasty breakers. The three boats bucked and rolled, sinking and
rising from the mud with each wave, and there was nothing we
could do but watch until the tide bottomed out, came back in,
and calm was restored. The cleanup was gross because my boat
had been thoroughly dunked in the filthy bay water, and I was
very shaken by how close I had come to losing her. What would
have happened in an anchorage with a rocky bottom?

That awful feeling kept me out of tide-related trouble for
eleven years, until a trip in Thailand and my second story. We
were three boats in a flotilla on our first night out from a charter base. Tired and cranky after a long day of provisioning, stow-
ing, checking in and meeting each other, we rode a tidal current
that carried us out to a cleft in a small island just as the sun was
setting. Three captains consulted three depth sounders and three

anchors were dropped in water that was deemed sufficiently deep.

Mosquitoes droned around my head, the windless night was stifling hot, and I wasn't getting much sleep anyway, so the sound of the keel rubbing on something hard in the wee hours didn't take long to register. I was on deck in a flash and in the feeble starlight, I could see the gleaming white hull of one of the other boats lying on her side and hear muffled voices of consternation drifting across the water. The tide had receded much too far and every time my boat swung shoreward on her anchor, we touched a coral head. I took the spare anchor and kedged us out a bit and cringed for what seemed like hours whenever we grazed the muddy bottom. At least we didn't end up on our side, the bottom was mostly mud, and tides always come back in. By dawn, we were all safely afloat again and sailing up to visit James Bond Island, where we took great care to anchor in plenty of depth.

I still don't know how tides work, but the ebb and flow of all this for the average sailor is that they do exist and they are a force to be reckoned with and considered, especially when traveling in unfamiliar territory. What I do know is that tables covering most places in the world have been calculated, tabulated, and extrapolated for the mariner and, thanks to them, we have all the information and predictions we need to take appropriate navigational action without needing to understand the cause behind every effect. So, next time the kids ask about tides, unless I've acquired another story, I'll pull a book of tide tables out of the same sailor's cap. That should turn the tide and reduce the flood of questions to a trickle, and I'll still come out looking as if I know something.

PART 8

Home Is the Sailor

Photo Ops

～～～

Seas and skies suffused with blues and greens of colorful crispness, exotic and foreign harbor architecture, natural attributes of sultry anchorages, and the highlights of flat calms and raging tempests have inspired even the least artistic of us to try and capture moment after perfect moment on film. Anybody who owns a camera and has done any kind of sailing knows what I'm talking about. Whether you've gone digital, or you're a professional photographer with thousands of dollars worth of equipment, or you're still using an old-fashioned point and shoot, here are a few scenarios that might sound familiar:

"Whoa. Look at the size of that wave! It's as high as the spreaders! Let me just crouch down into the cockpit here and get your face and backstay into the foreground for some perspective. Whoa, hang on!" Click.

Or . . .

"Hey, look at those awesome peaks. Bora Bora is something else. Won't I look good reclining on the bow pulpit with that background scenery? Here, take a picture of me from the dinghy. And, one more, please, over here, behind the wheel." Click.

Here's another good one:

"Guys, come look at this! The dolphins! Oh my God, they're so beautiful! They're all over the place! Wow, did you see that flip? Get me the camera, quick. I've gotta have pictures of this!" Click.

And, who can ever resist a rainbow?

"Aw geeze, could it get more gorgeous than this? The contrast of color, the whites of the sails, the turquoise water, the dark billowing clouds, the way the rainbow ends right in that cleft in the hills, the way it makes all the boats in the anchorage we're approaching seem so at peace after the squall . . . This one's gonna be a keeper." Click, click.

If you've spent any time at all on a boat, you're with me. And you're still with me (if you haven't been deleting the digital duds all along) when the film comes back from the developers, while the impressions of what you experienced are still fresh, and you flip the pictures in disbelief.

"Where's the big wave? It was at least twenty feet high; this doesn't look any more than three!"

Then . . .

"Is that me on the bow pulpit. Oh, man! I look like such a dork, and what's up with the thunder thighs? Why didn't you tell me I have turkey posture? Hey, you can't even see Bora Bora. You dummy, you let the boom get in the way!"

And . . .

"What are these blobs in the water? Oh yeah, the dolphins. Boy, was my timing off. They look like shadows. Oh, wait. Here's an okay one. You can see the tip of a tail just before it goes back under!"

And, where's the rainbow?

"There it is, sort of. I know the colors were much more vibrant in real life. The sails look washed out. And, how come the sky and water are almost the same color? This film sucks. That's what you get for buying the cheap stuff. And, I need a zoom lens. The boats in the anchorage are specks."

There might be one or two shots that begin to resemble what the scene meant for you, where the colors, the perspective, and the subject have come together into a nice composition. They're the ones you submit with the article, the ones you frame, or download onto the screen saver. Some of the others, pictures of friends, family, trees, flowers, or people you've met, make it to the photo album.

By and large, though, the pictures are disappointing, falling way flat of the postcard reality that prompted you to get out the camera. They can't harness the sound of the howling wind whipping up the gigantic wave that towered over you in all its three dimensional glory, before the crest splashed across the cockpit as the rest of it lifted and passed under the stern to make way for the next wall of water.

Maybe the magnificence of Bora Bora was contagious and it made you *feel* like a breathless Polynesian beauty, even though the railing was cutting uncomfortably into your butt while the picture was being taken. Now, you look kind of like you're unbalanced and about to fall overboard, nothing like the picture of the girl on the cover of that sailing magazine. Plus, not a single shot recaptures the stunning panorama you remember, only sections of it.

The same goes for the dolphins; the camera fails to seize the sound of the bow cutting through the water, the whistling of the graceful mammals speeding alongside, and the sensation of unbridled joy and freedom they brought to you. And the rainbow? Well, it's pretty enough, but what you can see of the lively cloudbank from which it emanated is lifeless, dismal and gray.

The pictures never take you all the way back to the original stirring moment. After the first rush of disappointment, time goes by, and you get over it. You realize, once again, you can never go back, nor will you ever earn a living from taking pictures, even if your sailing life is all about the dream material in coffee table books and magazines.

Years pass, old memories are replaced by new, and you keep upgrading equipment and attempting to preserve original, moving moments on film. You end up filling shoe boxes with the many pictures that don't make it to albums, frames, or slide shows, the flops you can't throw away because of some redeeming feature you want to remember—a building you liked, a friend, your child being cute, a jellyfish, a companion boat under sail. And, for what the archive is worth, it ends up being what keeps your memories alive, inasmuch as they can be kept alive.

The hint of a fish tail brings back that particular passage, the people you were with, perhaps even the events of that day, and it rekindles a bit of the exultation you felt when the dolphins came to cavort around the bow of your boat. The picture of the wave reminds you of the storm that taught you how well you could meet the challenge of an extreme, and the crewmate who freaked out and couldn't. Even your awkward youthful pose on the bow pulpit becomes endearing with revisited familiarity and nostalgia, because it was taken in Bora Bora, and what could be cooler than that?

If it weren't for the pictures, whatever the quality, you'd remember much less than you do, and if only for the memories, you are grateful. It makes the fact you look nothing like the siren on the cover of last month's issue of *Latitudes and Attitudes* more bearable. And, because she looks so good, you still whip out the camera at every opportunity, and keep trying. As long as the sailing life continues to be your visual muse, the hopeful artist in you won't give up.

Homecoming

Home is the sailor, home from the sea. If you're a sailor, you might already know this line is from Robert Louis Stevenson's poem, *Requiem.* Just in case you didn't know, Stevenson wasn't just the author of classics, *Treasure Island* and *Dr. Jekyll and Mr. Hyde* among them, but he was also a big sailor. Or, at least he became one toward the end of his life. He was a sickly guy, and several years before he died, because it was believed the tropical climate would do him good, he, his mother, his wife and her son, a French maid, and a revolving assortment of other crewmembers sailed away from San Francisco. For two years at the end of the late 1800s, in the same decade Slocum began his epic journey, the Stevensons looped around the South Pacific, zigzagging and dropping in for visits to all kinds of idyllic islands until they set anchor for the last time in Western Samoa. This is where the words to Stevenson's epitaph were immortalized on his tombstone. Ever since, sailors have been stepping back on their home shores, or onto the docks of places they have chosen to settle, echoing these four words with sighs of relief and regret: home is the sailor.

Of course, some misanthropic types want to be as far from other people as possible, and they have no use for land other than as a place for provisioning. But, mountaintops or the middles of deserts, not just boats, can accommodate this kind of characters. Most people sail into sunsets to enjoy them, or to simply survive, with the intention of coming back to a shore richer for the experience and to tell their stories. Why? Because the whole point of sailing is to get back to land, and when it is to come back to stay, these sailors become the flip side to those who keep cruising. They are the sailors who hang up their sextants and foul-weather gear, and go on to discover how some aspects of sailing and living aboard become the template for how we live anywhere.

For instance, years after you've run aground, you may find yourself flying over the Himalayas. Your plane hits an air pocket and drops far, very far, way further than any other plane has ever dropped, and passengers around you are screaming. Thanks to skills honed by living aboard, as the plane drops into the trough, you know instinctively to grab your tray and teacup, and they, and you, float in suspension until the plane rides back up the air-wave. On boats, you've learned that until other things become more important, things like life and death, you must always secure your food and drink.

Every time the mares tails come scudding in, followed by a relentless, water-table-replenishing deluge, and the roof doesn't leak, you don't take it for granted. You are grateful. When the wind howls, whipping around the house and tearing sheets of unlashed roofing tin off the woodpiles, knocking down trees and cutting out electricity, you take it over the bow while other people take it up the stern. You know how to light a kerosene or gas lamp, or how to fire up a generator, if you have one . . . and a jerry can of fuel to power it. If you don't have a gravity-fed well, you get out other jerry cans to go find some water. If you have a gravity-fed well, you know how to be thankful for a water source with no pumps to maintain, and you wait for neighbors to come fill their cans.

You hunker down, you are prepared for whatever happens because you know weather-related challenges, and you kind of like to be tested by them on land, where the extremes you suffer will never be as dramatic as they were at sea. Because the earth is solid underfoot, the rock you come back to when you're done floating, you say: bring on the snow, ice, and floods. You can handle them, and you always keep an eye turned to the sky, finding comfort in the fact that the only thing stable about it is change, as the sun moves from equinox to equinox.

You have learned home economics with the most unforgiving teacher, you know what it means to be far from buying that missing item, and you can't ever shake the need to always have stores on hand. You like to be prepared, and you know how to stock up so you can improvise with what you have. You have spare parts, tools, shovels, good snow tires, you change the oil on your car regularly, and you keep the windshield wiper fluid filled. You work out the systems that support you, you can troubleshoot many things, and nothing ever seems quite as dire as drifting out of a bay with only one oar in the dinghy and an outboard that won't start, God knows why not.

You listen for the wind, you keep track of the weather, and the sound of faucets left running always make you cringe. You hear and see snowmobiles carving up pristine white fields and they become jet skis churning up tranquil anchorages. You see litter on roadsides and remember your bow slicing through trashy slicks marring the perfect ocean blue. You know your garbage. On boats, you became intimate with trash and how much you generate, and you are never again so blithe about how many bags you haul to the dump or place curbside every week. You've seen people around the world make do with little, happily and well. You know the practicality and usefulness of things, and you know dead weight is heavy. You try to keep it to a minimum because if it weren't enough, it wouldn't be called the minimum.

You have learned about wakes, how to keep them clean, and you can't forget the song of the sea. You know and appreciate what it taught you, and this melody becomes part of your internal soundtrack. You can take the sailor far away from the sea, but you can never take the song of the sea completely away from the sailor, wherever home may be.

Picture This

Just stop. Stop long enough to imagine everything as still. Feel it, this stillness, all but the flapping of the triple-reefed mainsail catching as the boat under you rocks from side to side on the gentle swells. The ocean is never completely still, but it can get pretty close and you're there now. You're sitting in a cockpit, a cockpit that can be tailored to your own taste—a catamaran, an aft cockpit, a center cockpit. The boat can be big or small. Pick your pleasure. Your back isn't hurting, your butt isn't sore, you aren't wishing you could be down below, in bed, dreaming. None of that is happening because this is the picture-perfect perfect picture and it is yours.

A pastel dawn is just beginning to break out of twilight, the first rays of sun stretching its fingers and cracking its knuckles over the brim of the world, suffusing a faraway bank of low-lying clouds in peachy hues. If you study it closer, the edges of the puffy white columns glow with a golden light, the trimming on a royal robe cloaking the eastern horizon, spreading across the glassiness in great undulating and rippling whorls.

You are blissfully awed and comfortably alone. Perhaps you're single-handed, or you're alone on the morning watch while your family, friends, or strangers, or whoever became part of the circumstances that brought you to this juncture, are sleeping below. These details are on the periphery of the picture. Distractions. They don't really matter. The point is you are alone in the cockpit.

Look at the teak deck stretching away toward the bow, the long lines of wood and putty, but don't think about how the putty needs caulking. Don't focus on the spot where you know the leak above your book collection is coming from. Get past that, follow the straight lines forward to a vanishing point, the bow pulpit, and beyond, to the endless expanse of water around you.

It might be the Indian Ocean, the Atlantic or the Pacific—a precise location is irrelevant. All you need to think about is being several hundred miles along the way from somewhere, about a third of the way to wherever. In other words, you're in the middle of nowhere. You've just passed the night in the middle of nowhere, you're on watch, and another way to read "nowhere" is "now here," the only place to be at the dawn of a new day.

You're totally in the moment, the last harbor a memory, the next landfall a dream. It might have been a calm trip up until now, and using the engine still isn't an option since you need to conserve fuel. Or maybe, the engine isn't even working, and you're facing a day of doubling over greasy, smelly nuts, bolts and filters. Wait. Stop thinking like that. It could also be the calm after a spell of raucous trades, the break you've been hoping for, some down time before the wind comes back.

The boom swishes, pulling up short from one end of its mainsheet tether to the other, as the small bit of mainsail stops the boat from rolling too dramatically from side to side, keeping the sounds of clunks in lockers and cabinets out of this picture. Yes, somebody on this boat, maybe you, maybe another pair of hands now slumbering below, has reefed down the mainsail in the calm to minimize flapping and rocking, which is why everything feels so gentle.

Or, maybe the sail has to be reefed because it ripped ten feet along the second reef line just before the wind died last night and you're waiting for enough light to make repairs. But this doesn't matter either. You don't have to bring up the thought of needles and thread right now. It's just another one of those pesky peripherals. Look up past the sail, to the masthead as it scribes an arc in a sky above about to burst into full blue. The water laps, pushing and pulling away from the restless hull, slapping up against the transom.

The tendency to wax poetic about the sea is as old as language, but we won't think about water rushing in past waterproof bulkheads, or crashing on nearby reefs. We don't want any of those thunderously disturbing sounds here. Forget the HES-PERUS. Listen to this instead: splish splash, splish splash, lap lap. Ah, yes, this is good poetry.

Now, look up through the crosshairs of the bow pulpit, behind the jib. Look past the furling drum, to the zigzags of color alternating between dark and light tracing spirals across the water. You can see the small silhouettes of seabirds, resting before starting another day of whirling and swooping, harassing the schools of smaller fish navigating the treacherous terrain between birds preying on them from above and the bigger and hungrier fish below.

Just think. Between the sea floor and you are six thousand feet of water molecules, jostling each other and piggybacking down through the layers of light into unimaginable darkness, a place of lantern-bearing, big-toothed fish with exoskeletons and eyes as big as their entire bodies. Anything could be down there, an improbable monstrous creature of the deep, or a single molecule wandering in lonely eternity ever since Columbus tipped the dregs of his beer overboard. Maybe, two of the molecules that once shared this same cup are on a collision course, about to meet again after more than four hundred years. Right there. Under you. What a joyful reunion that would be, if you could believe molecules know joy.

So much could be happening below, unbeknownst to those on the surface. Tectonic plates could be shifting, new canyons and mountain peaks could be forming while the rain of silt keeps filtering down, covering it all in a blanket of clues to history. But what do you care? It's like that Calvin and Hobbes comic strip:

Test question: "What was the significance of the Erie Canal?"

Calvin: "In the cosmic sense, probably nil. We 'big picture' people rarely become historians."

A quartet of flying fish erupts, splashing through the mirrored stillness off the bow, gliding through the air in formation, up and away from something scary. Right here and now, you are in the big picture, aboard the microenvironment of a small boat in the macroenvironment of the enormous ocean. Here, you can be master of all and nothing. "Praise the sea, but keep on land," said the seventeenth-century poet and clergyman George Herbert. Then, he added, "He that will learn to pray, let him go to sea."

You prayed and here you are. Or maybe you didn't pray. Maybe somebody forced you to come along, but all that doesn't matter, either. Not in this picture. It is here only for now, an ephemeral moment to behold, and it's grand. Quick. Try to see it for yourself. The pleasure is all yours.

Fantasea

~~~~~~

I've become one of those sailors who lives ashore and dreams of sailing away again while lining up the obstacles and shooting them down—in my imagination. There isn't really very much in the way other than a divorce, two children who have a regular schedule with both parents, and the lack of about fifty thousand dollars. So, I try to come up with creative ways of dealing with the kid issue. We can trade years instead of weekdays, I think. If I get them for one year, their father can have them the next. Or, alone in the car, I practice asking him if I could just take them for the year and he'd be welcome to visit us whenever he wants. I haven't given him the chance to respond to either request, and the dashboard doesn't have much to say.

The idea of discussing this negotiation scares me more than any wave, driving me to quickly move on to imagining the boat, the efficient way I'd go about procuring one. What kind of boat would I get? Where would I get it? How would it be outfitted? These are the questions I have the most fun with, the kinds of problems I like to solve.

Back in the early nineties, my father was finishing up a desert-based adventure in Africa when he found himself swept up on the shores of Senegal, in the seaside city of Dakar, eying a steel cutter bobbing in the harbor with a "for sale" sign hanging from the rigging. Only five years old, it was basically a new boat, built in France as per the specifications of one couple's dreams. They had sailed down the European and African coasts and when they reached Dakar, they were faced with a choice. Either they could head even farther away from the home and families they missed, across the Atlantic to Brazil, before arcing back across the North Atlantic, a voyage of thousands of miles and many months. Or, they could sail back up the way they came, against the wind and currents, a shorter distance mileage-wise, but a much more difficult one weather-wise. Neither choice was appealing, so they found a third: sell the boat and fly home. The trouble was that in Dakar, the used boat market was pretty stagnant and they had been steadily lowering the price until my father came along. He ended up buying a 41-foot cutter for fifty thousand dollars, extensively equipped for a world cruise, tools and dinghy included. With his wife, my father sailed it across the Atlantic to the Caribbean, puttered up-island to Florida, and sold it there for a hundred thousand dollars.

In Florida, a man I met found a fully equipped aluminum boat that had been abandoned by another French couple for similar reasons. My friend bought it for something like thirty thousand dollars, and he went on to live aboard with his wife, raising a child, crossing more than one ocean, and gathering shells, langoustes, and stories for many years before our wakes crossed. These two are the tales I remember; there are many others I can't get as straight. With lots of inspirational examples, I figure my own chances of finding something suitable are good, better than winning at bingo.

Assuming I suddenly come into fifty thousand dollars and am given the requested year with the boys (for seamless and painless reasons I can't imagine so well), I could then become deliberate about the boat. The clock for the trip would have to begin ticking in December, so in the preceding months, I'd have to pack the car and drive down to Florida and the Gulf Coast. Starting on the east coast, I'd pick up local classifieds and read them in diners over breakfast sandwiches and tea, before each day of dock pounding, seeking brokers and "for sale" signs attached to lifelines. Down the Interstate and offshoots I'd drive, taking notes and gathering contact information for anything interesting, narrowing the options.

Maybe I'd bother with the Keys, maybe not, before swinging back northward up the west coast, across the panhandle toward Alabama, Mississippi, Louisiana, and perhaps even as far as Texas. Assuming my hankering to see some of these states is strong enough to keep me going past the first likely boat candidate in northeastern Florida or the Carolinas, this would be my chance to do some side trips into the countryside, to break up the monotony of fiberglass knocking and bilge crawling.

Along this coast, the used boat market will be a smorgåsbord of opportunity. I am sure of this. Without ever having seen it with my own eyes, I know there will be no shortage of marinas and boatyards down there, filled with current, abandoned, or washed up dreams. Boats and dreams, realized and broken, are inextricably linked, and I ought to be able to find my own shrink-wrapped match. There is no way I won't be able to find something in this used-boat world of opportunity for people standing in the right place at the right time with a suitcase of cash. My problem would be to fight off impulsiveness, an impatience for shopping, and to not buy the first boat "that'll do."

I used to think I wanted steel, but older and wiser, I've learned that to keep up with peeling paint trim on a house may be directly equated to keeping one step ahead of rust on a boat. The trim on my house is faded and peeling all over the place, and though I would never opt for vinyl siding, I think a fiberglass boat might be a better idea. Still, if an attractive steel or aluminum one were to pop up, it would not be discounted.

Fin keel or full keel? It doesn't matter, as long as the keel is well attached. Centerboard? Fine, as long as it is well attached, too. Kerosene or gas stove? Who cares? We can live with any heat source for a year. Refrigeration or not? Whatever. If the hull and rigging are sound, a good steak and fresh vegetables taste all the better after a period of going without. After all, the point of sailing off with my boys for a year would be to bring them into direct contact with simple needs. For just one year, the three of us together, home schooling, writing, and playing cards, sailing across the Caribbean and South Pacific, off another beaten path.

The boat only needs to last about nine thousand miles to New Zealand or Australia, where we could sell, keep, or give it away. Sloop or cutter, 32- to 36-feet would be a good size, something the boys, who are only getting bigger and stronger, and I, who am not, can handle easily enough. Good sails are preferable, because without them a sailboat is nothing but a major pain. It should also have hefty ground tackle, a couple hundred feet of chain and a fair bit of rode, because few things are more important than a good night sleep. And, of course, it must have a reliable self-steering system.

Yes. In my imagination, I get all this and everything else that needs to come with a pre-owned and equipped boat for under fifty thousand dollars. Once the boat is mine, I make haste to return home, pack up my charts, sextant, books, tools, GPS, and jerry cans. I grab the kids, our bathing suits, harnesses, and foul-weather gear, store some stuff, and rent out our fully furnished house, chickens and rabbit included, to pay its overhead and some of ours underway.

Yes. Then we'd have a year of staying a course, following the weather and seasons from landfall to landfall in an even bigger adventure I can only imagine.

For now.